**I wasn't able to express myself,
I just couldn't do that.**

CW00819214

PRISONERS' VOICES

Contents

Contents

I didn't know what was going on; I tried to take it in. They did their best.

Possible learning disabilities.

Acknowledgements

Over the last three years *No One Knows* has worked with, and been supported by, a large number of people – far too many to name individually. I am however extremely grateful to all of them for their wise advice, practical support and for the kindness they have shown towards me.

As with any programme of work, there are also a number of people whose involvement has been of particular significance and these are listed below.

- Members of the advisory group, in particular Baroness Joyce Quin who chaired the group; also Karen Bryan, Andrew Fraser, Glyn Jones and Glynis Murphy whose support went way beyond what could reasonably be expected.

- Members of the Working for Justice Group whose candid views and gritty questions kept things very 'real'; in particular Anthony Fletcher, Danny McDowell and Lee Owen.

- Mencap for being a partner organisation, in particular Jo Williams who provided much encouragment and valued guidance; Jo was also a member of the advisory group.

- KeyRing Living Support Networks, in particular Judith Atkinson and Tracy Hammond.

- For this study, *Prisoners' Voices,* special thanks to the prisoners who agreed to be interviewed – without their input this report would not have been possible; thanks also to the prison staff who made all the arrangements, to the prison governors for agreeing that the research could be undertaken at their prison, to Jon Mason for generously allowing the use of the LIPS screening tool, to my fellow researchers, to Dan Ahmed and Melanie Skerritt for their heroic efforts in data inputting and typing up interview scripts and to Sarah Capel and Charlotte Collard for their attentive proof reading.

- Nancy Loucks whose work has ensured that Scotland and Northern Ireland, as well as England and Wales, were integral to the *No One Knows* programme, and who has been a valued colleague.

- Jessica Jacobson whose reports on the police and the courts have added greatly to the work of *No One Knows*.

- The following people have provided much support and encouragement at various points throughout the programme: Isabel Clare, Janet Cobb, Wendy Goodman, Merron Mitchell, Greg O'Brien, Lis Pritchard, Dora Rickford, Chris Riley, Wendy Silberman, Roger L. Taylor and Paul Thornton.

And finally thank you to my colleagues at the Prison Reform Trust.

The Prison Reform Trust is very grateful to The Diana, Princess of Wales Memorial Fund for its generous support of *No One Knows*.

Foreword

As a former Minister for Prisons in the Home Office I was very aware that there were people in the prison system who had learning disabilities and learning difficulties. I knew, too, that many of them struggled to make sense of their experience of imprisonment. However it has been through my close involvement with *No One Knows*, as chair of its advisory group, that I have become more fully informed about the sheer numbers of people affected and how often their needs are not properly met or understood, not just in prison but throughout the criminal justice system.

Indeed it has to be a matter of deep concern to all involved in seeking to improve our criminal justice system that in this report, notwithstanding mentions of good practice and decent treatment, many prisoners recount harrowing experiences at police stations, courts and prisons. It seems that, compared with prisoners without such impairments, people with learning disabilities and learning difficulties are more likely to experience depression and anxiety and to be subject to bullying and be less likely to have opportunities to address their offending behaviour or to progress their sentence.

This final report of the *No One Knows* programme sets out clear systematic recommendations as well as a blueprint for local action. The clarity and precision of this excellent piece of work typifies the way in which the report's author Jenny Talbot has managed the *No One Knows* programme from the start. Over three years, the Prison Reform Trust, generously supported by The Diana, Princess of Wales Memorial Fund, has succeeded in making initial improvements to, amongst others, screening for learning disabilities, commissioning services, staff training and the inspection of the treatment and conditions of prisoners. Following engagement with *No One Knows* a number of prisons have begun to adjust their regimes to take account of the particular needs of prisoners with learning disabilities or dificulties.

I would like to express my personal warmest thanks to Jenny for her exceptional management of this complex programme of work. I would also like to say how grateful and appreciative I am of the help and expert guidance which has been so readily provided by the members of the advisory group throughout the duration of the programme. I hope and trust that the publication of this report will mark the start of a thoroughgoing implementation of our recommendations across a range of Government departments and the devolved UK administrations. Now that *everyone knows*, no one can be in any doubt about how much needs to be done to address the needs of people with learning disabilities or difficulties and in a way which not only gives them greater opportunity and justice but also helps to improve the situation in the criminal justice system overall, and to the benefit of society as a whole.

Joyce Quin, House of Lords
Chair, advisory group, *No One Knows*

Summary

This report presents the findings of a major survey of prisoners with learning disabilities and learning difficulties, which explored their experiences of the criminal justice system. Drawing on the survey, and earlier research by *No One Knows*, the report concludes with a discussion of five over-arching themes from the three year programme and a series of recommendations.

No One Knows is a UK-wide programme run by the Prison Reform Trust that aims to effect change by exploring and publicizing the experiences of offenders with learning disabilities and learning difficulties who come into contact with the criminal justice system. The work is guided by people with learning disabilities who have been in trouble with the police, and professionals and academics from health and social care, learning and skills and criminal justice. *The No One Knows* programme is chaired by the Rt Hon Baroness Quin, former prisons minister for England and Wales. A number of reports and briefing papers have been published by *No One Knows* and these are shown at appendix 1.

The report is in four parts:

Part one describes the aims of this study, *Prisoners' Voices*, and methods used. The overall aim was to document the experiences prisoners with learning disabilities or learning difficulties have throughout the criminal justice system in order to highlight areas for improvement. The involvement of prisoners without such impairments has enabled comparisons to be drawn.

Semi-structured interviews with prisoners yielded qualitative and quantitative evidence. Quantitative data were logged on SPSS and analysed to obtain frequencies and cross-tabulations.

Prisoners were identified by prison staff and 173 agreed to be interviewed, all of whom were asked to undertake a screening tool for learning disabilities. Screening tool results suggested that 34 prisoners had possible learning or borderline learning disabilities. A further 73 prisoners were identified as also likely to experience difficulties with verbal comprehension skills, including difficulties understanding certain words and in expressing themselves.

Part two tells of prisoners' experiences of the criminal justice system, their lives immediately before they were arrested and aspirations for the future. It also includes a section on prisoners' ideas for change.

Before being arrested: prisoners were almost twice as likely as the comparison group to have been unemployed. Over half had attended a special school and they were three times as likely to have been excluded from school as the comparison group.

At the police station: less than a third of prisoners received support from an appropriate adult during police interview and half of prisoners with possible learning or borderline learning disabilities said they didn't know what would happen once they had been charged. A few said they had been beaten or handled roughly by the police and felt manipulated into agreeing to a police interview without support.

In court: over a fifth of prisoners didn't understand what was going on in court; some didn't know why they were in court or what they had done wrong. Most prisoners said the use of simpler language in court would have helped.

In prison: most prisoners had difficulties reading and understanding prison information, which often meant they didn't fully understand what was going on or what was expected of them. They also had difficulties filling in prison forms, which for some meant missing out on things such as family visits and going to the gym, or getting the wrong things delivered such as meals. Over half said they had difficulties making themselves understood. Prisoners frequently had difficulties accessing the prison regime, including offending behaviour programmes, and spent long periods of time on their own with little to do. However, over half of prisoners said they attended education classes and those with possible learning or borderline learning disabilities were the most likely to say so.

Prisoners were five times as likely as the comparison group to have been subject to control and restraint techniques and were three times as likely to have spent time in segregation. Over half said they had been scared while in prison and slightly less than half said they had been bullied; none of the comparison group said they had been bullied. Prisoners were almost three times as likely as the comparison group to have clinically significant depression or anxiety.

Thinking about their futures, prisoners expressed a wide and varied range of aspirations, including finding work, going to college and re-building their lives. However most had unrealistic expectations about the type and extent of help they might receive from statutory services. Prisoners with possible learning or borderline learning disabilities were the least likely to say they had somebody to help them make plans to prepare for release and were the most likely to say they had worries about leaving prison and that they might come back.

When asked for their suggestions of how things might be improved, over half had positive ideas for what might help.

Part three presents and discusses five overarching themes from the three year *No One Knows* programme, which are:
- disability discrimination and possible human rights abuses
- knowing who has learning disabilities or difficulties
- implications for the criminal justice system
- a needs led approach: collaborative multi-agency working
- workforce development.

Two further issues are discussed, which are:
- diversion from the criminal justice system of people with learning disabilities
- children with learning disabilities or difficulties and statutory education.

The likely 'double discrimination' of black and minority ethnic people with learning disabilities or difficulties who offend is noted and the requirement for further research made.

A concluding discussion draws attention to the high levels of discrimination experienced by people with learning disabilities or difficulties as they enter and travel through the criminal justice system, and the failure of the UK criminal justice agencies to comply with disability and human rights legislation.

Part four draws on the full three year *No One Knows* programme and makes recommendations for change. Local check lists for action are included at appendix 9.

The recommendations include:
- the requirement for UK criminal justice agencies to comply with disability and human rights legislation
- the need to know who has learning disabilities or difficulties as enter the criminal justice system in order that appropriate action may be taken
- the need for effective and reciprocal information sharing between criminal justice agencies, health, social services and education
- the development of a needs led approach and mandatory multi-agency working at the local level to help prevent offending and re-offending by people with learning disabilities and difficulties
- workforce development, to include awareness training on learning disabilities and difficulties and increased capacity of specialist provision
- the development of alternatives to custody, in particular for people with learning disabilities
- national standards for health and social care provision
- clarification on methods and criteria for fitness for police interview, and the concept of criminal responsibility as applied to people with learning disabilities
- greater precision in terminology, in particular 'mental disorder' and 'vulnerable'.

Introduction

No One Knows is concerned with people with learning disabilities and learning difficulties who enter the criminal justice system, their experiences as they travel through it and in particular the effect their impairments have on their ability to cope with the exigencies of the criminal justice process.

Over the last two and a half years *No One Knows* has consulted with professionals and practitioners from criminal justice, offender health and social care and offender learning and skills; undertaken relevant literature and policy reviews and a number of reports have been published and early recommendations made, see appendix 1.

This study hears directly from prisoners themselves.

Hitherto comparatively little was known about the numbers and needs of people with learning disabilities or difficulties caught up in the criminal justice system; however it is a matter that has long troubled those who manage criminal justice services, in particular the staff who work directly with such prisoners. As one member of prison staff said in research previously undertaken by *No One Knows*:

`Working with people like this is time consuming and is not resourced adequately; it is often the case that it conflicts with performance targets, for example adapted programmes` (for prisoners with learning disabilities or difficulties) `take longer to run and therefore it is harder to reach targets. The key issue is getting everyone adequately assessed on reception so that we can manage them appropriately all the way through their sentence. Many are good at being able to function without anyone suspecting they have difficulties, for example they have learned vocabulary to use but don't understand it.`

A literature review undertaken by *No One Knows* shows that:
- 20-30% of prisoners have learning disabilities or difficulties that interfere with their ability to cope within the criminal justice system

- *this group of prisoners:*
  - o are at risk of re-offending because of unidentified needs and consequent lack of support or services
  - o are unlikely to benefit from programmes designed to address offending behaviour
  - o are targeted by other prisoners when in custody (Loucks, 2007).

Further, criminal justice staff will often not know which people have learning disabilities or difficulties — theirs is largely a 'hidden disability' with few obvious visual or behavioral clues.

The underlying assumption of this study is that, because of their impairments, people with learning disabilities, and to a lesser extent those with learning difficulties, will be made vulnerable by a criminal justice system that neither recognizes nor supports their needs, so creating particular difficulties with regard to peoples ability to understand and to participate fully in the process to which they are subject. The potential for wrongful conviction and non-compliance with disability discrimination and human rights legislation has far reaching consequences should this assumption be proved.

This report:
- describes the experiences of the criminal justice system by prisoners with learning disabilities and learning difficulties
- discusses five overarching themes from the three year *No One Knows* programme
- draws on earlier research by *No One Knows* and presents recommendations for change.

Summary versions of this report for the four UK nations, and an 'easy read version', are available.

Background

No One Knows is a three year, UK-wide programme run by the Prison Reform Trust that aims to effect change by exploring and publicizing the experiences of people with learning disabilities and learning difficulties who come into contact with the criminal justice system. The work is guided by two advisory groups and is chaired by the Rt Hon Baroness Quin, former prisons minister for England and Wales. The advisory groups bring two very different perspectives to the work of *No One Knows*. The Working for Justice Group comprises members with learning disabilities who have been in trouble with the police and who were able to talk about relevant issues from their own experience; the second advisory group comprises professionals and academics from the statutory and voluntary sectors, all experts in their own fields, from health and social care, learning and skills and criminal justice. Members of the Working for Justice Group and the advisory group are shown at appendices 2 and 3.

What do we mean by learning disabilities and learning difficulties?

It was by no means straightforward deciding what, for the purpose of the *No One Knows* programme, was meant by 'learning disabilities and learning difficulties'. This fundamental question would determine who would benefit from the research and, by implication, who would not. Definitions of learning difficulties and learning disabilities used for research purposes with offenders vary widely and include strict 'medical model' definitions based on IQ as well as wider 'social' definitions that include a range of impairments and other difficulties (Loucks, 2007).

The World Health Organization (WHO)[1] defines learning disability as a 'reduced level of intellectual functioning resulting in diminished ability to adapt to the daily demands of the normal social environment.'

IQ levels are given as a guide and the range 50 – 69 'is indicative of mild mental retardation', or mild learning disability. Variations on this definition are followed by the four UK administrations all of which stipulate that an IQ below 70 is not of itself sufficient to diagnose learning disability and that impairments of social functioning and communication skills should also be present.

However, many people with an IQ of 70 and above will also experience major difficulties with understanding and communication. These may include, for example, people with speech and language difficulties, people with attention deficit and attention deficit hyperactive disorders, people with dyslexia and people on the autistic spectrum, including Asperger syndrome.

In her research, McBrien noted that (2003):
One of the most prevalent vulnerable groups amongst prisoners comprises those who do not have an intellectual disability as formally defined but who have much lower cognitive and adaptive abilities than do either the general population or the offending population.

In deciding who to include *No One Knows* also took account of the Disability Discrimination Act (DDA). For the purpose of the Act, whether a person is disabled is generally determined by reference to the effect that a particular impairment has on an individual's ability to carry out normal day-to-day activities. The impairment must be physical or mental and have adverse effects that are both substantial and long-term (DDA guidance, 2006). While it is not possible for DDA guidance to list all conditions that qualify as impairments, the examples given include dyslexia, autistic spectrum disorders and learning difficulties/disabilities.

No One Knows has purposefully not adopted precise definitions of learning disabilities and learning difficulties that would serve to either include or exclude people by a very fine margin. That said there are occasions where precise definitions and diagnosis are important. For example, for people with learning disabilities a diagnosis of learning disability is often required to invoke relevant legislation and policy frameworks, including access to service provision, and where appropriate this has been highlighted.

1. ICD-10 Guide for Mental Retardation, World Health Organisation, 1996

Learning disabilities and learning difficulties:

No One Knows has included in its scope people who find some activities that involve thinking and understanding difficult and who need additional help and support in their everyday living. The term learning disabilities or difficulties thus include people who:

- experience difficulties in communicating and expressing themselves and understanding ordinary social cues
- have unseen or hidden disabilities such as dyslexia
- experience difficulties with learning and/or have had disrupted learning experiences that have led them to function at a significantly lower level than the majority of their peers
- are on the autistic spectrum, including people with Asperger syndrome.

People with learning disabilities are not a homogenous group, neither are those with learning difficulties or those on the autistic spectrum. They are all individuals with a wide range of different life experiences, strengths, weaknesses, and support needs. However many will share common characteristics, which might make them especially vulnerable as they enter and travel through the criminal justice system. A number of these characteristics are described at appendix 4.

The terms learning disability, meaning intellectual disability and learning difficulty are often used interchangeably; in this report they are not.

Prevalence of offenders with learning disabilities or difficulties in the criminal justice system

Research undertaken to determine prevalence rates shows a wide variability in estimates, which is due to a number of factors including which screening and assessment tools were used, the stage in the criminal justice process at which screening or assessment was undertaken, whether assessments were conducted individually or in groups and the level of training of the people administering the assessments (Loucks, 2007).

Recent studies show that:

- 20 – 30% of offenders have learning disabilities or difficulties that interfere with their ability to cope within the criminal justice system (Loucks, 2007)
- 7% of prisoners have an IQ of less than 70 and a further 25% have an IQ of less than 80 (Mottram, 2007)
- 23% of prisoners under 18 years of age have an IQ of less than 70 (Harrington and Bailey et al, 2005)
- 20% of the prison population has a 'hidden disability' that 'will affect and undermine their performance in both education and work settings.'(Rack, 2005)
- dyslexia is three to four times more common amongst prisoners than amongst the general population (Rack, 2005)
- there is a small over representation of those with autistic spectrum disorder in the special hospital population (Hare, Gould, Mills and Wing 1996); prevalence in the prison population remains unclear.

Despite a lack of clarity on prevalence and how best, methodologically, prevalence might be determined, it is clear that high numbers of people with learning difficulties and learning disabilities are caught up in the criminal justice system.

For the purpose of this programme, prevalence rates demonstrated by an extensive review of literature undertaken by *No One Knows* have been adopted. These show that 20-30% of offenders have learning disabilities or difficulties that interfere with their ability to cope within the criminal justice system (Loucks, 2007).

Context
UK administrations

Responsibility for criminal justice, offender health and social care, and offender learning is the responsibility of different UK administrations. In brief:

England and Wales: responsibility for prisons, probation and criminal law and justice lies with the Ministry of Justice; court services are the responsibility of HM Court Services, which is an executive agency of the Ministry of Justice; responsibility for policing lies with the Home Office.

England: the responsibility for offender health is shared in a partnership between the Ministry of Justice and the Department of Health; responsibility for offender learning lies with the Department for Innovation, Universities and Skills, managed through the Learning and Skills Council.

Wales: responsibility for offender health and offender learning lies with the Welsh Assembly Government, Departments for Health and Social Services and for Children, Education, Lifelong Learning and Skills respectively.

Scotland: responsibility for prisons, police, criminal justice social work, legal profession, anti-social behaviour, courts and law reform lies with the Scottish Government Justice Directorate; responsibility for prisoner education lies with the Scottish Prison Service as does prisoner health[2].

Northern Ireland: responsibility for operational issues associated with policing and criminal justice including prisons, lies with the Northern Ireland Office; responsibility for the Northern Ireland Court Services lies with the Ministry of Justice; responsibility for offender learning lies with the Northern Ireland Prison Service, responsibility for offender health lies with the Northern Ireland Assembly, Department of Health, Social Services and Public Safety.

Relevant consultations and reports

Although there have been a number of consultations and reports from UK administrations that have focused on people with learning disabilities and learning difficulties, content relating to people with learning disabilities or difficulties who offend is limited. Two recent exceptions are:

- *A Life Like Any Other? Human Rights of Adults with Learning Disabilities,* the report of an enquiry into the human rights of adults with learning disabilities by the Joint Committee of Human Rights[3] (2008), which included a section on 'accused and defendants' with learning disabilities and to which *No One Knows* submitted evidence.

- Bradley review[4]: the Secretary of State for Justice (England and Wales) announced a review into the diversion of prisoners away from prison in December 2007. Lord Keith Bradley, former Home Office Minister, was appointed to chair the review under the following terms of reference:

To examine the extent to which prisoners with mental health problems or learning disabilities could, in appropriate cases:

- *be diverted from prison (the criminal justice system) to other services, the barriers to such diversion; and*

- *to make recommendations to government, in particular on the organization of effective court liaison and diversion arrangements and the services needed to support them.*

Lord Bradley has consulted widely, including with both advisory groups for *No One Knows* and is expected to report in December 2008.

Another government consultation, *Improving Health, Supporting Justice,* looked at how health and social care services can be improved for people subject to the criminal justice system in England. Uniquely, the consultation took an holistic view and was a joint initiative between the Department of Health, Department of Children, Schools and Families, Ministry of Justice and the Home Office. Between them, these government departments/agencies have responsibility for health, social care and all the component services with in the criminal justice system (Department of Health website, October 2008). The consultation report and subsequent strategy will follow publication of the Bradley Review. The Prison Reform Trust responded to the consultation, including evidence gathered by *No One Knows.*

Disability Discrimination Act (DDA)

The amendments to the Disability Discrimination Act 1995 made by the Disability Discrimination Act 2005 introduced the Disability Equality Duty (DED). The DED has both general and specific duties.

The *general* duties, which public authorities are required to meet, are to:
- promote equality of opportunity between disabled persons and other persons
- eliminate discrimination that is unlawful under the DDA
- eliminate harassment of disabled persons that is related to their disabilities
- promote positive attitudes towards disabled persons

2. The Prison Health Care Advisory Board has considered re-configuration with the NHS commissioning and providing healthcare to prisons (see Prison Health in Scotland, 2007)
3. The Joint Committee of Human Rights is appointed by the House of Lords and the House of Commons to consider matters relating to human rights in the UK
4. Although the consultation has involved stakeholders in Wales the final report will apply in England

- encourage participation by disabled persons in public life
- take steps to take account of disabled persons' disabilities, even where that involves treating disabled persons more favourably than other persons.

Unlike the *general* duties, not all public authorities are required to meet the *specific* duties, which are effectively steps to help authorities to achieve the general duty; they are the means to an end rather than the end themselves. Importantly the specific duties require the production of a Disability Equality Scheme (DES), which provides the level of specificity and timescale needed to ensure that progress is made.

While authorities such as the police and local government are required to meet both the general and specific duties, including the production of a DES, prisons (including contracted out prisons) and the courts are required only to meet the general duties. This contrasts strongly with the position of other public bodies such as schools and NHS hospitals, which are required to produce an individual DES. For England and Wales, the Ministry of Justice is required to meet both the general and specific duties and as such produces *one* DES for all prisons and courts.

Clearly, the production of one scheme will, necessarily, be very general. For example, one scheme for 142 prisons in England and Wales will not be able to go into sufficient detail to ensure that disabled prisoners in their care are not discriminated against and receive equality of opportunity.

Similarly, in Scotland, the Scottish Prison Service has one DES and although it covers a much smaller number of prisons (15), it nevertheless makes it much harder to hold individual establishments to account.

Moreover the lack of a DES for individual prisons removes any commitment to a timescale for action.

Inclusion agenda

The principle of inclusion of people with disabilities in society was enforced by the revision in 2005 of the DDA. The inclusion of the DED was a major change in equalities legislation as it required most public authorities to be proactive in taking action to mainstream disability equality throughout their organization and services rather than leave equality as a 'bolt on' extra.

The DED has the dual aim of eliminating discrimination and promoting equality, thus public authorities must work to ensure that discrimination does not occur by, for example, making adjustments to existing service provision and in ensuring that future provision is accessible to people with disabilities, including some people with learning disabilities and learning difficulties.

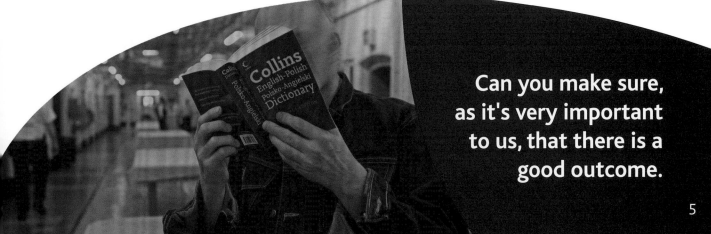

Can you make sure, as it's very important to us, that there is a good outcome.

Structure of this report

This report is presented in four parts:

PART ONE: Aims and Methods.

This section describes the aims of this study, *Prisoners' Voices*, and methods used.

PART TWO: Prisoners' Voices.

This section describes prisoners experiences of the criminal justice system and includes their lives immediately prior to arrest and aspirations for the future.

PART THREE: Conclusion.

This section presents main findings from this study and discusses five overarching themes from the three year *No One Knows* programme. Two further issues are discussed and the need for additional research noted.

PART FOUR: Recommendations.

This section draws on findings from this study and the three year *No One Knows* programme and makes recommendations for change.

To be honest if you're someone like me they treat you like shit, a piece of dirt. My dad is not an MP, my mum isn't clever. I'm just a nobody and people can do what they like.

PART ONE

Aims and Methods

I didn't like not understanding anything...

Young offender

Aims of this study

The primary aims of this study were to:

✳ hear from prisoners identified by prison staff as having learning disabilities or learning difficulties about their experiences of the criminal justice system

✳ highlight the implications of prisoners' experiences for the criminal justice process: that is the extent to which their learning disability or difficulty may impede due process, and where prisoners' experiences are reduced in quality and opportunity as a direct consequence of their impairments

✳ inform the recommendations for change.

Secondary aims were to:

✳ compare the experiences of prisoners with learning disabilities and learning difficulties to those of prisoners without such impairments.

Note: although this study covers prisoners' experiences of the criminal justice system, including at the police station, at court and in prison, experiences of probation or criminal justice social work were not included solely on the basis of their being insufficient time to cover everything during interviews with prisoners; the greater focus of this study is on prisoners' experiences in prison.

Methods

Prison staff were asked to identify prisoners who, in their opinion, had learning disabilities or learning difficulties and whose first language was English; they were asked to say whether the prisoner had learning disabilities or learning difficulties and whether any diagnostic screening or assessment had been undertaken. A small number of prisoners who, according to prison staff, did not experience such impairments were also interviewed. These 19 prisoners – the comparison group in this report – were intended to provide:

• qualitative evidence which could be used to illustrate ways in which prisoners with learning disabilities or learning difficulties experienced the criminal justice system; and

• quantitative findings which could be similarly used.

Quantitative data from the interviews with prisoners were logged on SPSS and analysed to obtain frequencies and cross-tabulations. The relatively small size of the comparison group meant that cross-tabulations rarely achieved high statistical significance (in this report, the p value will be cited as appropriate). Further, the selection of the comparison group was based on a judgment by prison staff that the offender did not have learning disabilities or difficulties, and individual members of staff responded to this request in different ways.

Methods used

The interviews were semi-structured involving both qualitative, open-ended questions and quantitative, closed questions. A number of line drawings were available for researchers to use during interviews to assist prisoners in responding to questions. Prisoners were also asked to complete:

- LIPS, learning disability screening tool[5], see appendix 5
- Glasgow Anxiety Scale for people with an Intellectual Disability[6]
- Glasgow Depression Scale for people with a Learning Disability[7] .

Procedure

The research was undertaken between May and November 2007 and took the form of one to one interviews with prisoners from England and Wales and Scotland. Participating prisons were identified, and invited to take part, to reflect the prison estates in England and Wales and in Scotland. Identification took into account levels of security, the age and gender of prisoners, and mix of public and contracted out establishments.

Information about the research was available for prisoners in 'easier to read' versions. The consent form, which all prisoners signed, was also translated into 'easier to read'. Prisoners were invited to take part in the research by a member of prison staff; participation in the research was voluntary. In all but one interview the researcher interviewed the prisoner alone. Each interview lasted for around one and a half hours including breaks as required.

A total of 173 interviews were conducted at 14 prisons; ten of the prisons were in England and Wales and four were in Scotland. Of this group:

- 154 interviews were conducted with prisoners identified by staff as having learning disabilities or difficulties (this group will, on occasion, be referred to as the target group); staff described slightly under half of this group as having learning disabilities and slightly over half as having learning difficulties

- 19 interviews were conducted with prisoners who, according to staff did not have learning disabilities or difficulties (this group will be referred to as the comparison group).

Prisoners were identified by a range of different staff including from education, IAG (information, advice and guidance), psychology, healthcare and, in Scotland, speech and language therapy, and prison officers. A smaller number of prisoners were referred from workshops and prison industries and some were self referrals. Most prisoners were identified by education staff (37%), followed by prison officers (22%) and psychology (17%).

Fewer than half of prisoners in the target group had undertaken any screening or assessment to determine the likely presence of either learning disabilities or difficulties. Where a screening tool or assessment was used, most prisoners were identified on the basis of results from the Basic Skills Assessment[8]. Smaller numbers were identified through different assessment or screening tools for dyslexia, or by WAIS-111, and in Scotland an alerting tool was used, see table 1.

Table 1: assessment or screening tool used by prison staff to identify learning disabilities and difficulties:

Screening tool or assessment used	%
None	42
Basic skills assessment	19
Dyslexia, various	8
WAIS-111	8
Alerting tool (Scotland)	4
Other)	2
Data missing	17

Ethical considerations:

The research was based on the Ethical Principles of the British Psychological Society (Robson 1993) and the British Educational Research Association (revised 2004). The consent form and information about the research were trialed with people with learning disabilities prior to being used to help ensure that prisoners taking part in the research were able to give informed consent to being interviewed. Participation was strictly voluntary and prisoners were reminded of this at the start of the interview.

---

5. No screening for learning difficulties was undertaken
6. See J. Mindham & C. A. Espie; Journal of Intellectual Disability Research, volume 47 part 1, pp22-30, January 2003
7. See Fiona M. Cuthill, Colin A. Espie and Sally-Anne Cooper; British Journal of Psychiatry (2003), 182, 347-353
8. The Basic Skills Assessment is used by education staff in prison to determine levels of ability in particular with regard to literacy and numeracy. While the assessment determines levels of ability, it does not identify underlying causes; it is an assessment rather than a diagnostic tool. However education staff will often use the basic skills assessment to help to identify difficulties that prisoners have with their learning, taking into account preferred learning styles and previous experiences of education (Talbot, 2007).

Prisons have not been named to preserve the anonymity of prisoners and prison staff.

Permission:

Permission to undertake this research was given by the Prison Service (Efficiency, Strategy and Research Section) in November 2006, reference: PG 2006 062 and the governors of the individual prisons visited.

Research team:

The research team comprised eight experienced researchers, led by Jenny Talbot, author of this report, see appendix 6.

Nobody told my mum I was going to gaol, she thought I was dead. I asked how they were going to tell my mum, but it took three months for anyone to contact her. I finally found someone to help me write a letter.

Scotland, possible learning disabilities.

PRISONERS'VOICES

PART TWO

Prisoners' Voices

I just worked. I worked for the council, I did litter picking. There are gangs doing it on the motorways, I had the job for two months.

Young offender, possible learning disabilities

Prisoners' profile

A profile of the prisoners interviewed, including the results of the LIPS screening tool is at appendix 7

Throughout this section reference is made to prisoners with possible learning disabilities, possible borderline learning disabilities and, to a lesser extent, prisoners with possible low average IQ. These descriptions are based solely on the results of the LIPS screening tool rather than identification by prison staff. The word 'possible' is used because in the absence of a full assessment whether a person has learning disabilities, is borderline or low average IQ remains uncertain. The sole exception to this is where, at one of the prisons, healthcare staff confirmed the diagnosis of learning disability for one of the prisoners.

Quotes from prisoners are identified as follows:

- women prisoners, young prisoners (up to and including 20 years of age), the comparison group and prisoners from Scotland are identified as such

- prisoners who screened positive on the LIPS are identified as either having 'possible learning disabilities' or 'possible borderline learning disabilities'. Note: prisoners identified as having possible learning or borderline learning disabilities are an integral part of the target group

- where no identification is made, the prisoner is male, from the target group and is being held in the prison estate for England and Wales.

...I'm not a dull lad, I may have ADHD and can't concentrate but I'm not dull.

Young offender

Before being arrested

Although primarily concerned with prisoners' experiences of the criminal justice system, this report also includes the daily living experiences of prisoners immediately prior to their arrest. This section looks at how prisoners spent their time before they were arrested, who they lived with, whether they cared for or supported anyone at home or received support themselves. While most prisoners had left full time education some time ago, they were also asked about their experiences of school.

What did prisoners do during the day before they were arrested?

Around a quarter of prisoners were in full time employment and more than half of the comparison group was. A small number of prisoners attended college or day centres and undertook voluntary work:

Well I didn't work. I've got a dog and I used to look after her and I went to Touchstone, it's not a drop in centre but it's good. I can make my own lunch there, you can do your washing and drying and that's where Keith and Liz are, they are my support workers.
Woman prisoner, possible learning disabilities

I was working doing labouring. I was going to probation three times a week and they were going to set me up with a cooking course. I moved to x (next town) sorting myself out but they came and nicked me. I can understand that as I'm appalling on paper but now I am really trying and I've got character references. I'm not a dull lad, I may have ADHD and can't concentrate but I'm not dull.
Young offender

What were prisoners living arrangements before being arrested?

Less than a third of prisoners lived with a partner or a partner and children and a just over a fifth lived with one or both parents or on their own; around one in ten were homeless prior to being arrested. The comparison group were more likely to live with a partner or a partner and children and none were homeless.

What was a typical day?

Prisoners were asked to describe a typical day prior to being arrested. Responses ranged from being in full time employment and with a happy family life through to chaotic lifestyles, unemployment and drug and alcohol abuse. An analysis of qualitative data suggests that many prisoners experienced troubled lives prior to being arrested;

• Drug and alcohol abuse

Around a quarter were regularly involved in drug and/or alcohol abuse:

I used to take drugs, roam around the streets just trying to find things to do.
Young offender, possible learning disabilities

There were lads bullying me on the outside. I was smoking cannabis but they bullied me into doing what I did and they got me slashed at x prison. I had a good job, I was labouring and had some factory work, I was a bin man, I've had loads of jobs. But when I started smoking cannabis I ended up owing money and then I started to get bullied. I will never smoke again, it has ruined my life and it's not good for you.
Possible learning disabilities

• Tough lives and family problems

Slightly under a fifth described troubled lives and family problems; several had been a 'looked after' child. Yet there were differences within the target group; prisoners with possible learning or borderline learning disabilities were less likely than others to describe their lives in this way:

I was homeless and stayed in a bed and breakfast, it was shit. I had been off drugs for nine years but moved onto alcohol. I'd spend my money on alcohol and scrounge off other people's dinner plates for food I was taken into care at the age of four through till I was 16. I was sexually abused at 14 by the babysitter and that really threw me off the rails. Scotland, possible learning disabilities

I had nowhere stable to live, I stayed here and there. My ex-husband used to make trouble and my kids were in care. I didn't have a job and no college place.
Woman offender

I was homeless and an alcoholic as I was
mentally abused at home; they told me I
wasn't wanted and that they didn't love me. I
was struggling, I wasn't working at all. I
got no outside help. Asked by the researcher what might
have helped? I needed more support before I
actually got into that situation.

I was living in a shelter, just drinking
and thieving. I was in care from about
four years old, I don't remember my home.
After leaving the children's home I got a
job at Safeway. When I was there I went
to stay at my dad's and sister's for a
week, but it didn't work out I don't see
my mum; I'm not sure where she is. When I
left the children's home that is when I
got into crime. Young offender

• Doing nothing in particular

Slightly less than a fifth said they did nothing in
particular during the day, although for some it wasn't
for want of trying. Young prisoners were the most
likely to describe their lives in this way and no one in
the comparison group did:

I have been on benefits ever since I was
a little kid. I filled in a form for
McDonalds but I never got an interview. I
did painting but that was an illegal
business. Young offender, possible learning disabilities

I would look for a job; I didn't get into
trouble on the outside. I was on income
support, but I wanted a job but careers
said I was incapable of working. They
gave me a test but I couldn't do it. I
used to have black outs and they put me
on valium. Young offender, possible learning disabilities.

I did bricklaying and gardening part
time. I was on benefits sometimes as I
couldn't get a proper job because I
couldn't read or spell. Then just before
I got arrested I got a job in a factory
filling dolls and soft toys.

Did prisoners receive any help or support before they were arrested?

Just over half of prisoners said they received help or
support before they were arrested. Prisoners with
possible learning disabilities were the most likely to
say they received support.

Support came from social workers, care support
workers, GPs, parents and other family members,
special friends, probation officers and for one prisoner

from a community nurse. Support received by
prisoners with learning disabilities or difficulties was
most likely to be 'formal', for example from a social
worker or a care support worker.

Did prisoners care for or support anyone before they were arrested?

Prisoners were asked if they helped to support or care
for anyone, including looking after a pet and over half
said they did. Prisoners were most likely to say they
cared for one or both parents, followed by their
partner and/or their children. Prisoners with possible
learning or borderline learning disabilities were the
most likely to say they cared for a pet and none said
they had children to care for. The comparison group
were most likely to say they cared for their partner
and/or their children and none said they cared for
their parents.

What did prisoners think about school?

Prisoners were asked whether they enjoyed school
and those with learning disabilities or difficulties were
more than twice as likely as the comparison group to
say they did not, 48% and 22% respectively.

• What prisoners said about school, good things:

I enjoyed school because you got to do
anything you wanted; you could go to the
shop at playtimes.
Scotland, young offender, possible learning disabilities

I loved school. I went to a backward
school between age six and eleven.
Woman prisoner

The teacher was good, helped to explain
things that I didn't get. The people were
nice, I had friends too.

• What prisoners said about school, bad things:

At first I went to mainstream school,
then two months into year eight they
tricked me and my mum, they wanted to
send me to a special school on a trial
basis but they wouldn't let me back and
from there my life went mad. I started
bunking off and stealing cars.
Possible borderline learning disabilities

I went to a special needs school, there
wasn't any help there and that was hard.
You don't fit in with people and you
can't get a job therefore crime just
seems easy.

I was bullied at school; I was left handed, plus I was diagnosed with dyslexia. That may have been a reason as to why I didn't like school.

I didn't like not understanding anything.
Young offender

I went to a special school; I was very unconfident and struggled with spelling and maths. When I got things wrong I just shouted.

• Neither good nor bad:

I didn't learn anything from school, the only thing I learnt was to have a lot of days out on coaches to Thorpe Park, swimming and camping for example. There were a lot of activities when we went away but not so much learning on how to read and write for people who had learning difficulties. I was at school from seven to sixteen years old and I still couldn't read or write when I left.

I went to an ordinary school up until I was eight years old and then I went to slow school. It was alright there, it was for people who couldn't read or write.

• A small number of prisoners said they hadn't been to school:

I never went to school; I stayed at home to care for my disabled mother until she died when I was 15. After that I just hung around with my friends and got wasted. Scotland

I didn't go to school; a tutor came to the travellers' site. We used to all love it. Young offender

• More about growing up than going to school:

I never had a great upbringing like other kids who had shiny new shoes, I never had that. I always felt like, 'why should I learn?' Scotland

It was better being at school than being at home, my mum was a drug abuser and she was always in bed. She never made any tea. Woman prisoner

I went to x secondary school but I was kicked out of there. I went into care, went to different foster homes and secure units. I then went to a special school it was like a bad behaviour school, but after that I hardly went to school. I never seemed to settle down anywhere. When my dad left home the family fell apart, there was no routine and my mum fell apart and went off the rails.

I was only there for a year then I got put in a special school. I then went back to school for three months; I tried to burn the school down and I was put into care I was always getting suspended for fighting.

Attendance at a special school and extra support in mainstream school

Over half of prisoners said they had attended a special school at some point during their education, which rose to almost two-thirds for those with possible learning or borderline learning disabilities; a further one in ten said they had received extra support while attending a mainstream school. A number of prisoners said they had attended 'bad schools' for behavioural problems and pupil referral units. One prisoner in the comparison group said they had attended a special school and two said they had received extra support.

Exclusion from school and playing truant

Prisoners with learning disabilities or difficulties were three times as likely to have been excluded from school as the comparison group, 51% and 17% respectively and this was statistically significant ($p = 0.004$).

Almost three quarters said they had played truant and over half of the comparison group said they had. Prisoners with possible learning or borderline learning disabilities were slightly more likely to have played truant and to have been excluded from school than other prisoners.

Being ullied at school

Over one in three prisoners said that they had been bullied at school; prisoners with possible learning or borderline disabilities were least likely to say they had been bu lied.

It was scary, shameful, you feel ashamed of yourself. I think the whole thing is scary.

Arrest and at the police station

There are various safeguards in criminal justice and policing policy aimed at protecting the general welfare of vulnerable suspects, facilitating their access to treatment and support where appropriate and reducing risks of miscarriages of justice that could arise from their vulnerability (Jacobson, 2008).

Initial arrest

Prisoners were asked about their experiences of being arrested, including 'what was it like, how did you feel?' Being arrested is always likely to be a stressful experience and as one prisoner said:

I don't think anyone is happy when they are arrested.

All prisoners shared negative experiences. An analysis of qualitative data showed that:

• Around a third used words like scared, frightened, terrible, awful, 'not nice' and confused to describe their experiences, which increased to over half for those with possible learning or borderline learning disabilities:

I was shaking; it was just scary, very scary. Scotland, possible learning disabilities

It was awful, I cried all the time, I couldn't stop being sick, I was totally frightened. Woman prisoner

I was scared; I didn't know what would happen. I was just walking down the street, I had a gun in my pocket, not a real one, and it fell out.

It was really scary. I was confused because I thought they were there for my ex rather than me. I asked for my mum, but they said I wasn't allowed. They kept rabbiting on with all these big words and I didn't know what was happening. I was afraid they were going to come in the cell and do something to me. I had been beaten and raped by my partner so I was scared. They wouldn't give me a cigarette or anything. Woman prisoner, Scotland

One young offender was so affected by the experience he had a panic attack:

I woke up in hospital as when I got arrested I had a panic attack so I collapsed.

- Around one in five prisoners said they were either too drunk or high on drugs to remember what it was like when they were arrested. However, no prisoners with possible learning or borderline learning disabilities said this.

- Around one in ten said they were beaten or handled roughly by the police[9]. No prisoners in the comparison group said this had happened to them. Young prisoners were the most likely to say they had been beaten or handled roughly:

I was quite intimidated. They gave me a 'doing' and I felt I was being mistreated. Possible learning disabilities, Scotland

The police beat you really bad.
Possible borderline learning disabilities

They were rough with me and made me stay outside in the cold for about an hour and a half. Woman prisoner

- Smaller numbers of prisoners, slightly fewer than one in ten, said they felt relieved:

I was relieved because I don't mind going back to gaol; there's nothing for me to do outside. Young offender, possible learning disabilities

I had set myself up to get caught; I wanted to get caught as I needed the attention and the help. I was very intoxicated at the time. I felt scared but also relieved. Scotland

To be honest I was quite relieved. I feel that I have had a problem all my life, but I can cover it up quite well. I turned up drunk at the door with a mallet in my hand to speak to a guy and I wondered to myself, if the guy had actually been in, I might have argued with him and would have hit him and killed him.

- Smaller numbers, fewer than one in ten, all of whom had possible learning disabilities, said they didn't know what it felt like when they were arrested or couldn't remember:

I don't know, I was half asleep when I got arrested because it was only 9 o'clock. They said to me, 'do you remember this? Do you remember that?' I said 'no'. Young offender, possible learning disabilities

One prisoner couldn't remember because she had a fit at the time of her arrest:

I woke up when I was getting put into the cell, they took me to hospital as I had another fit, then I went to court.
Woman prisoner, possible learning disabilities

- Smaller numbers of prisoners, fewer than one in ten, said they were looked after or treated fairly. However no prisoners with possible learning or borderline learning disabilities said this:

It was traumatic because I self harm and the cell door had to be kept open. The officers were fine and looked after me.
Woman prisoner

- Five prisoners said they were suicidal, thought about self harming and self harmed. No prisoners in the comparison group said this happened to them:

I wasn't happy. They don't like me, I don't like them. I asked for my medication[10] and they said I couldn't have it. I warned them, I said I didn't want to live anymore. I was in self destruct mode. Possible learning disabilities

I self harmed, but it was my own thing, it wasn't their fault.

- Two prisoners, one with possible learning disabilities said they were denied their medication:

When I was arrested I said I needed my medication[11] and they left it for three days and then even when I went to court I didn't have my medication and I was shaking and my solicitor was going mad.
Woman prisoner

9. See also PRT submission to the Joint Committee on Human Rights, The Human Rights of Adults with Learning Disabilities, call for evidence, June 2007
10. ibid
11. ibid

She must have thought I was really bright, she used big words and just expected me to understand them. She expected me to tell her things I couldn't really tell her.

Woman prisoner

- One prisoner said he felt he was being manipulated[12]:

> They say to me, 'if you want an interview we can do it now or you can wait five hours for a solicitor to come'. You don't want to wait that long to be interviewed. They do the same with a caution, you have to plead guilty and then you can go, but you feel pressured to plead guilty.

Support during police interview

Prisoners were asked whether there was anyone other than a police man or woman or a solicitor to help them understand what was happening when they were interviewed by the police. Just under a third said there was somebody present to help and around a tenth of the comparison group said so.

Help came from family members, support workers, friends and appropriate adults; one prisoner said help came from a sign language interpreter, others received help from a drugs worker, a Scottish Association of Mental Health (SAMH) worker and a police doctor.

Of those who said they had received support, over a third said it came from somebody previously unknown to them; no one in the comparison group said this.

Despite there being a 'helper' present, it wasn't always clear what support, if any was actually given during the interview:

> I had my support worker there, she just sat there, she didn't help, she was there for her own good, not mine. Young offender, possible learning disabilities

> My nana was there but she didn't speak. Woman prisoner

> A SAMH worker was there but he just sat there, he didn't explain anything. Scotland

One prisoner wasn't certain whether the people present at his interview were there to help him or not:

> There was a solicitor, one police lady and two other people. I don't know why they were there, police talk maybe. It was somebody I didn't know before I got in trouble with the police. I didn't know if it was someone who could have helped me.

One prisoner thought he could have either an appropriate adult or a solicitor, but not both:

> If I didn't have a solicitor, I could have had an appropriate adult. I thought it would be more beneficial to have a solicitor.

Help from a solicitor

In Scotland, despite there being no entitlement to legal advice at the police station, around a third said they received help from a solicitor and less than a fifth of the comparison group said they did.

One prisoner from Scotland, with possible learning disabilities, said she knew of her right to a solicitor from watching the television:

> I asked for a lawyer, I watch 'The Bill' so I knew I was allowed one but they wouldn't give me one. Woman prisoner

Over four-fifths of prisoners in England and Wales said they received help from a solicitor; prisoners with learning disabilities or difficulties were slightly less likely to say they received help than the comparison group. Prisoners with possible learning or borderline learning disabilities were the least likely to say they received help from a solicitor.

Prisoners who said they received help from a solicitor were asked in what ways the solicitor had helped. An analysis of qualitative data showed that prisoner perceptions of help received from solicitors varied.

Of those who said they had received help, over a third said they had been helped a lot. Help received was largely concerned with understanding what was happening, particular terminology and general welfare:

> He helped me by listening and directing me. He also stopped them if they went over the limit. Possible learning disabilities

> The solicitor sat and talked to me as long as I needed him, he was locked in the cell with me and I told him I was scared. Scotland, possible learning disabilities

   12. See also PRT submission to the Joint Committee on Human Rights, The Human Rights of Adults with Learning Disabilities, call for evidence, June 2007

They made them stop the tape and
explained everything to me; there was a
lot I didn't understand. Young offender

The solicitor read everything to me and
explained everything. He was really good.
Woman prisoner

The solicitor helped me to understand the
questions. He said them in a different
way so I could understand.

Just under a third of prisoners said the help they
received was more or less what they expected, no
more and no less and more than four-fifths of the
comparison group said this.

Around a fifth were 'unimpressed' with the help they
received. In the main, prisoners were 'unimpressed' if
they didn't feel that solicitors helped with their
understanding of what was happening, if they saw a
number of different solicitors, and if solicitors used
words they didn't understand:

A legal aid man represented me but I
didn't trust him. I saw four or five
solicitors. Possible borderline learning disabilities

They got me a dodgy solicitor who wasn't
my choice; he just sat there.
Possible learning disabilities

Two prisoners, both young offenders with possible
learning disabilities didn't think they needed any help
as long as they told the truth:

I didn't ask for any help. I told the
truth so I didn't need any help. I didn't
lie, I told them the truth.

What happens next?
Prisoners were asked if, once they had been charged,
they knew what would happen next. Around two-
thirds of prisoners said knew what would happen next,
which reduced to one half for those with possible
learning or borderline learning disabilities:

I had no idea.
Woman prisoner, possible learning disabilities

I didn't know I was charged, they didn't
read me my rights. I didn't know what was
happening. Young offender, Scotland

I didn't really know; I knew court would
come, and then they refused me bail. They
don't tell you anything; it was really
fast moving.

Good or bad things
Finally with regard to experiences at the police
station, prisoners were asked if anything good or bad
had happened to them. Around a fifth of prisoners
said that something good had happened to them,
which reduced slightly for those with possible learning
disabilities.

• Good things that happened
Seemingly small things such as being treated kindly,
given refreshments or being able to take a shower or
go out for a cigarette featured a lot when prisoners
talked about 'good things' that had happened to
them:

I had some left over food and was offered
a shower and some tobacco.
Scotland, possible learning disabilities

They made me feel very welcome.

The officer in charge was a nice guy. One
policeman actually shook my hand.

They let my mum bring me some food.
Young offender

They gave me a cup of tea, they knew I
was upset.

They took my fingerprints, I liked that
bit.
Woman prisoner, possible learning disabilities

I got a pot noodle.

Everyone who arrested me called me by my
first name.

One prisoner with possible learning disabilities said
that a 'good thing' was that:

the police never beat me up.

• Bad things that happened

40% of prisoners said bad things had happened to them at the police station and they were four times more likely than the comparison group to say so

In addition to prisoners saying that 'everything' was bad about being at the police station, an analysis of qualitative data suggests the 'bad things' that prisoners said happened to them can be clustered into five areas:

- *general conditions*
- *being scared, not understanding what was happening and acts of unkindness or thoughtlessness by police officers*
- *personal hygiene*
- *alleged brutality*
- *self harm and thoughts of suicide.*

Of those who said 'bad' things had happened to them:

General conditions
Around one in five talked about the poor conditions in which they were held, including being cold, not receiving any food or food being inadequate and not being allowed any exercise or opportunity to smoke a cigarette:

I only had one blanket and it was cold and the food generally wasn't very nice.
Scotland, possible learning disabilities

Being scared, not understanding and acts of unkindness or thoughtlessness
Slightly less than one in five talked about being scared, not knowing what was happening to them and being treated unkindly:

Three officers were making mad noises at me through the spy hole, calling me a boot head.   Young offender, possible learning disabilities

They were trying to scare me, saying I would get ten years and stuff like that.
Woman prisoner, Scotland, possible learning disabilities

The way they looked at you was scary. When you go up to the counter in the custody suite lots of people watched and they read out your charge. People look at you and then you are allowed to leave.

Personal hygiene
Smaller numbers, fewer than one in ten, said they had not been able to have a shower or clean clothes:

I was there for two and half days and I didn't have a shower. There was no toilet either; you had to press a bell, I nearly wet myself a few times. Woman prisoner

Alleged brutality
Smaller numbers, around one in ten, once again described instances where they had been beaten or handled roughly; none of the comparison group said this.

After the police beat me up I felt fine.
Young offender, possible learning disabilities

They manhandled me and were really aggressive.

Self harm and thoughts of suicide
Four prisoners spoke again about hurting themselves or having thoughts about suicide; none of the comparison group said this.

I tried hanging myself; they found me when I was blue. Woman prisoner

When asked if anything bad had happened to him at the police station, one prisoner said:

To be honest if you're someone like me they treat you like shit, a piece of dirt. My dad is not an MP, my mum isn't clever. I'm just a nobody and people can do what they like.

At Court

There is a general recognition in law that defendants must be able to understand and effectively participate in the criminal proceedings of which they are a part. The requirement for effective participation is reflected also in criteria used to determine 'fitness to plead', namely that the defendant can plead with understanding, can follow the proceedings, knows a juror can be challenged, can question evidence, and can instruct counsel (Jacobson with Seden, forthcoming).

Going to court

I couldn't really hear. I couldn't understand but I said 'yes, whatever' to anything because if I say, 'I don't know' they look at me as if I'm thick. Sometimes they tell you two things at once. Young offender, possible borderline learning disabilities

I didn't like it, it shocked me. The judge asked me if I understood and I said yes even though I didn't. I couldn't hear anything, my legs turned to jelly and my mum collapsed.
Young offender, possible learning disabilities

Prisoners were asked about their experiences of going to court. An analysis of qualitative data found that:

· Around a third used words such as stressful, nerve wracking, anxious, scary, frightening, shocking, and horrible to describe their experiences, which rose to over half for prisoners with possible learning or borderline learning disabilities:

I was scared. On the fourth day they charged me and the van came for me.
Learning disabilities (healthcare)

It was scary because I just see this man and two women sitting on a great big bench and I was in a glass box and there were all these others looking. A man then came over and said he was my solicitor but he was different from the one the night before. I thought to myself, 'what is going on?' Woman prisoner

It was weird. The court was big and there are lots of people, people could just walk in off the streets. I didn't know who they all were. Woman prisoner

> ## I understand that I have done something wrong, but I'm still not quite sure as to what that is.
> **Woman prisoner, Scotland**

I just felt sick. You go backwards and forwards. In court the psychology woman said I was like a kid. I can talk to people and I like people around but I don't think they realized that I couldn't read and write very well. They said I had learning difficulties.

· Just over a fifth said they didn't understand what was going on or what was happening to them. For some 'not understanding' seemed to relate more to process, while for others it was the use of language that prisoners found hard to understand. Smaller numbers of prisoners said they didn't understand why they were in court or what they had done wrong, and some said that on receiving their sentence they didn't understand that it meant being sent to prison:

I just felt out of place, being in court, that's the only way I can explain it. Everyone was talking; I didn't know what was going on. Possible learning disabilities

To be truthful, I couldn't understand them. They talk so fast, they were jumping up and down saying things. I gave up listening.
Young offender, possible learning disabilities

I didn't understand really, I pleaded guilty straight away. I didn't know what he meant when he said 'custodial'. Young offender

I didn't know what was going on and there's no one to explain things to you. They tell you to read things and in court you can't just ask for help. The judge thinks you can read and write just because you can speak English.

It's just that I didn't understand anything. Young offender

One prisoner didn't understand why he was in court:
I was upset; I didn't know why I was there. I really didn't think I had done anything wrong.
Young offender, possible learning disabilities

And another, although she knew she had done wrong didn't know quite what:
I understand that I have done something wrong, but I'm still unsure as to what that is. You also feel small when you are in court. Woman prisoner, Scotland

Three prisoners, one of whom was in the comparison group, said that on receiving their sentence they didn't understand that it meant going to prison:
I got sent to prison, which I didn't even know. Woman prisoner

I didn't understand. I didn't know what was happening. The reception prison officer at the prison explained.
Comparison group

• Less than a fifth of prisoners said they felt 'OK'. Feeling 'OK' included those with previous experience of being in court and who knew what to expect, prisoners who appeared to take it in their stride, and others who seemed ambivalent:

It was just like every other time I have been to court. It's a waste of time basically. Young offender, possible learning disabilities

It's just routine, I knew what was happening. I usually plead guilty straight away. I don't get bail anymore.
Scotland

Help in court
Prisoners were asked if there was anyone in court who helped them to understand what was happening. In

Scotland, defendants may have a 'supporter' in court, somebody whose role is similar to that of an appropriate adult at the police station.

England and Wales: almost three-quarters said they received help in court and around half of the comparison group. Prisoners with possible learning or borderline learning disabilities were the most likely to say they had received help.

Scotland: over four-fifths of prisoners said they received help in court and the entire comparison group.

Prisoners who said they did receive help in court were most likely to say they received help from a solicitor. Around a fifth of prisoners said they received help from a family member, and smaller numbers, less than a tenth, said they received help from a friend, a social worker, a probation officer and two said they received help from NACRO.

Prisoners were asked what sort of help they received, which they described, in the main, as being moral support and help with understanding what was happening. Moral support tended to come from family members and friends and help with understanding from solicitors.

• Moral support:

I had a family member with me. They helped by just being there.

My mum just explained; she made sure I was treated right.

I had my foster mum there, she was like my appropriate adult really. Young offender

• Help with understanding what was happening:

The solicitor chatted to me and told me not to worry. I was confused by all the adjournments, the solicitor and barrister explained.

The solicitor argued for me in court and explained things afterwards. Woman prisoner

The solicitor told me what was going on as I couldn't understand half of it.
Young offender

Some prisoners were ready with their praise for the help that solicitors had given:

```
I knew I was in for arson but all I did
was light a curtain to get a bit of
attention The solicitor did me proud She
also got me out of going to a nutty
prison. I don't know where I would be if
it wasn't for her. I would have killed
myself.
```
Possible learning disabilities

However even when the solicitor tried to help, it wasn't always productive:

```
The solicitor tried to talk to me but
used big words and I found it difficult
to understand. The solicitor came and
spoke to me in the cell and when she left
I thought, 'what was all that about?'
```

Additional support for prisoners with particular needs

One prisoner described how there were sign language interpreters in court because he had a hearing impairment, as did the victim:

```
There were four sign language
interpreters because the victim was deaf
also. They also helped me to talk to my
solicitor in private.
```

Two other prisoners were not so fortunate:

```
I explained in the car to my solicitor
about my speech, as I have a bad stutter.
I didn't give evidence because of that;
as if I'm nervous it begins to get worse.
I should have given evidence as my
solicitor didn't tell the judge
everything that I wanted him to say.
```
Young offender

```
Because I have special needs I can't just
send a note to my QC, and so I was
stuffed if I didn't agree with what they
were saying.
```

Good or bad things

Prisoners were asked if anything good or bad had happened to them while they were in court: over half said that bad things had happened and around a fifth said that good things had happened; prisoners with possible learning or borderline learning disabilities were most likely to say that something good and that something bad had happened to them.

• Good things that happened

When prisoners talked about 'good things' that had happened to them their responses were similar to the 'good things' they described happening to them at the police station; seemingly small things featured a lot such as being treated kindly, seeing familiar faces and being given refreshments:

```
The judge was alright; he didn't get
angry or shout. He was nice and polite.
```
Young offender, possible learning disabilities

A solicitor asked me if I knew what was happening.
Scotland, possible learning disabilities

```
They asked me if I wanted a cup of tea or
coffee. Later they asked if I wanted
something to eat. He was being kind to
me.
```
Possible learning disabilities

```
I got to see my mum and sisters while I
was there.
```
Young offender

```
I got to see my social worker and I drove
past my house on my way to court.
```
Young offender

• Bad things that happened

When asked about 'bad things' that had happened the most likely response was receiving their sentence and being sent to prison. A smaller number said 'everything' was bad and others singled out specific instances:

```
Some of the guys attacked me.
```
Scotland, young offender, possible learning disabilities

```
There was a long wait for the van to
collect me.
```
Scotland, woman prisoner, possible learning disabilities

```
I had a panic attack while I was there.
```

Other 'bad things' that prisoners talked about can be clustered into three areas:
· *Not understanding what was happening to them*
· *Difficulties in expressing themselves and feeling rushed*
· *Thoughts of suicide and self harm*

Of those who said 'bad' things had happened to them:

Not understanding what was happening to them
Around a fifth said they didn't like not being able to understand things; none of the comparison group said this.

The judges don't speak English; they say these long words that I have never heard of in my life. Young offender

I sat behind the glass and there were three ladies sitting there. I didn't know what 'remanded' meant. I thought it meant that I could come back later.

Difficulties in expressing themselves and feeling rushed
Around one in ten said they found it difficult to express themselves and needed more time. None of the comparison group said this:

I wasn't able to express myself, I just couldn't do that. Possible learning disabilities

I am not good at speaking and they don't listen. I needed more time to explain myself.

Thoughts of suicide and self harm:
Four prisoners said they self harmed or thought about self harming and suicide:

That's when I first tried committing suicide, but I didn't go deep enough.
Learning disabilities (healthcare)

I cut my wrists in the cells at the crown court; that's the only bad thing.

I tried to commit suicide in court. I had just had enough of life.

For one prisoner the 'bad thing' he described concerned his mum:

Nobody told my mum I was going to gaol, she thought I was dead. I asked how they were going to tell my mum, but it took three months for anyone to contact her. I finally found someone to help me write a letter.
Scotland, possible learning disabilities.

Being sent to prison

Finally in this section prisoners were asked how they felt when the judge or magistrate said they had to go to prison. Unsurprisingly, prisoners mostly used words such as 'gutted', stunned, upset, shocked, scared, 'bad', worried and depressed to describe their feelings. Smaller numbers felt 'OK' or didn't care and some felt relieved. A small number said they felt suicidal and one self harmed while at the court.

An analysis of qualitative data showed that:
· Around half of prisoners felt 'bad' about being sent to prison:

It was so hard. I was crying. I don't know what prison was like. Now I'm here, it's not life. Possible learning disabilities

I was really upset and I started getting angry and had to be put in a separate cell to calm down.
Scotland, possible learning disabilities

I was upset, I didn't like the judge. I wanted to go home with Stephen my boyfriend. I cried.
Woman prisoner, possible learning disabilities

I was very scared. I thought I was going to get battered.
Scotland, young offender, possible learning disabilities

· Just over a fifth said they felt 'OK' about going to prison: some felt they deserved a prison sentence; some had anticipated being sent to prison and had 'prepared' themselves for the eventuality; some said it was 'normal', part of life, and others said they weren't bothered:

I just say well if I have to go I have to go. I just felt hurt.
Scotland, possible learning disabilities

I knew I was going to prison so I just went with the flow because all my mates are in prison too.
Young offender, possible learning disabilities

I wasn't bothered; I was already here on remand. They all knew I couldn't read; it's a big disadvantage. They played me like an idiot.

- Smaller numbers, just under one tenth, said they didn't feel anything; it took a while for the sentence to sink in. One prisoner said she was still coming to terms with it four years on.

- Nine said they felt some relief at being sent to prison. Of this group, two had possible learning or borderline learning disabilities and two were in the comparison group. Seven of the nine were young offenders:

I felt I had nothing, I was stressed about it (coming to prison) but happy I could get off the drugs, I knew I would be coming off them by going to prison. I really need help in here; I see them (CARAT[13] team) every week and I told them about my problems.
Young offender, possible learning disabilities

13. Counseling, assessment, referral, advice and throughcare

It felt good to be honest because I was on heroin on the outside and I know me being inside for six months would help me to get off the heroin, which gives me another chance on the outside. Young offender

In a way I was glad because I was proper drunk a lot of the time, falling out with my family and that I needed to sort my head out. Young offender

- Two prisoners said again that they thought of suicide and both hurt themselves:

I felt really suicidal again. I cut my wrists again. They wrapped a bandage around my wrists and sent me to x prison.

I felt that it was the end of my life. I tried to kill myself. I tried to set fire to myself.

In Prison

Prisons are generally busy and noisy; they are run according to routine and prison rules. There are a number of factors that impact on prisoners experiences of life in prison, four of which are briefly described below:

- Overcrowding: prisons across the UK are experiencing overcrowding. At the end of September 2008, 89 out of 142 prisons in England and Wales were overcrowded (NOMS (2008) Monthly Bulletin – September 2008, London: Prison Service); on 24 October 2008, 13 out of 15 prisons in Scotland were overcrowded (personal communication with the SPS, 29 October 2008). Overcrowding means a higher proportion of prisoners to staff and fewer opportunities for staff to devote time to prisoners who may need support. See also PRT briefing, *Titan Prisons: a gigantic mistake.*

- Movement of prisoners around the estate: prisons receive large numbers of people from the courts on a daily basis, some of whom are remanded into custody while others are starting their sentence. Prisoners are regularly moved around the prison estate; sometimes moves are pre-planned and undertaken for a particular reason and at other times prisoners are moved with little or no notice and for no apparent reason. This 'churn' disrupts the routines, relationships and activities of prisoners, which can be particularly problematic when, for example, a prisoner is part-way through an education course. Continuity can be very important for people with learning disabilities in particular, so frequent moves may cause such prisoners especial hardship.

- Suicide: in 2007 there were 92 apparent self-inflicted deaths among prisoners in England and Wales; the suicide rate for men in prison is five times greater than that for men in the community; one study found that 72% of those who committed suicide had a history of mental disorder (Bromley Briefings, June 2008); in Scotland predisposing factors for suicide are evident in about 80% of the prison population (Scottish Prison Service).

- Mental health: 72% of male and 70% of female sentenced prisoners suffer from two or more mental health disorders (Bromley Briefings, June 2008); in Scotland 70% of prisoners are known to have mental health problems, and as many as 7% may have psychotic illness – a rate seven times higher than in the general population (Inspectorate of Prison for Scotland, 2006).

I have told them I need help but they don't pay any interest in me.

Levels of depression and anxiety in prisoners

Prison is a distressing experience for most prisoners and many will inevitably feel depressed and/or anxious at various points during their time in prison. The extent to which prisoners experienced depression and anxiety was measured using the Glasgow Depression Scale (GDS-LD) for people with a learning disability and the Glasgow Anxiety Scale (GAS-ID) for people with mild intellectual disability.

The same cut offs were used for people with possible learning disabilities and for those without such impairments. The cut offs for each of the scales was 15; each scale was validated against people who had a clinical diagnosis of depression or anxiety.

Depression

Seventy-four prisoners (52%) from the target group (people with learning disabilities or difficulties) scored above the cut-off for depression, i.e. they probably had clinically significant depression, compared to three prisoners (19%) from the comparison group.

In addition, the average scores for depressive symptoms were significantly higher for the target group than for the comparison group, see table 2.

Depression scores, table 2:

GDS-LD				
	Minimum score	Maximum score	Mean	Standard deviation
Target group (n = 142)	2	30	15.68	7.592
Comparison group (n = 16)	0	21	8.38	6.141
Possible LD or BLD[14] (n = 34)	4	32	16.59	7.943
The results between the target and comparison groups were statistically significant: t = 3.7; p <0.001				

Anxiety

Eighty-three prisoners (70%) from the target group people with learning disabilities or difficulties scored above the cut-off for anxiety, i.e. they probably had clinically significant anxiety, compared to four prisoners (25%) from the comparison group.

In addition, the average scores for anxiety symptoms were significantly higher for the target group than for the comparison group, see table 3.

Anxiety scores, table 3:

GAS-ID				
	Minimum score	Maximum score	Mean	Standard deviation
Target group (n = 118)	2	48	20.13	9.752
Comparison group (n = 16)	3	43	13.19	11.577
Possible LD or BLD[15] (n = 34)	8	41	16.59	8.804
The results between the target and comparison groups were statistically significant: t = 2.6; P = 0.010				

Anxiety and Depression

Fifty one prisoners (43%) from the target group scored above the cut-off for anxiety and depression, compared to three prisoners (19%) from the comparison group. Anxiety and depression mean scores are shown below at graph 1:

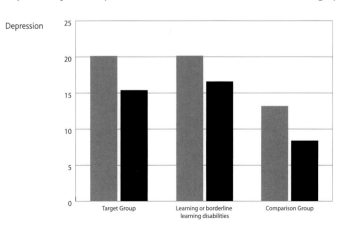

---

[14] Learning disabilities or borderline learning disabilities

[15] ibid

What is prison like?

Prisoners were asked what prison was like for them. For many it was hard, stressful, scary, depressing and lonely, some said they felt unsafe; others made of it what they could, taking each day as it came, and some were ambivalent. A small number had more positive things to say about being in prison and some said they preferred being 'inside' than 'out'.

Bad things about being in prison

Most described prison in negative terms and for some it was very hard:

It's scary, very scary.
Scotland, possible learning disabilities

It can be tough. There are issues with bullying and sexuality which can cause problems from inmates and staff. I have managed to get a single cell now.
Scotland, possible learning disabilities

It's not very good; the prison officers are not very nice to you such as the way they speak to you.
Woman offender, possible learning disabilities

It's hard, hard dealing with the sentence let alone dealing with the stresses of not being able to do the course.[16] The pressure of just being here and the pressure of having to do all the shit and knowing that you'll have to be here longer because you can't read is hard.

I feel lonely. I feel all alone.

It's been a nightmare. Basically I don't know what the rules and regulations are. When you come in they give you a huge induction pack and tell you to look at it, you don't get any help. I have told them I need help but they don't pay any interest in me.

A number of prisoners talked about missing their family; their mum, dad, partner and children:

To be truthful it's not very nice. It's just being away from my mum and dad; she's always on the phone crying. Young offender, possible learning disabilities

The worst bit is being away from my wife and daughter. Scotland, possible learning disabilities

At first it was horrible. I couldn't write to my family, I couldn't fill the sheets in (visiting forms) so my family wouldn't be able to visit. Nobody explained it to me. Young offender

I feel very guilty because I have children who are aged two, 14 and 15. I also have a grand-daughter with neuro-developmental degenerative disorder. I worry all the time. Woman prisoner

Smaller numbers, slightly fewer than one in ten, and one from the comparison group said they felt better being in prison than out:

Sometimes I feel I am better in here than when I'm out. I rely on my family a lot on the outside, so my family aren't under stress when I'm inside. How can I stop doing crime if I can't do anything? They might as well lock me up for longer than 17 months. Young offender, possible learning disabilities

Me, at the end of the day, me, myself, I prefer prison. You can't drink, you can't do drugs, you don't get into trouble. You don't have to pay rent and you don't have to buy food. I have trouble budgeting and you don't do that here. For me prison is like a big family. Don't get me wrong, I would be willing to work but now I have been inside it's hard to get a job... Don't get me wrong, how can I put it, 'would you employ me?' Young offender

---

[16] This prisoner was unable to progress through his sentence plan because the cognitive behaviour treatment programme he was required to complete demanded a level of literacy that he did not have; he was on an indeterminate public protection sentence, IPP, which means that until (and unless) he was able to demonstrate a reduction in risk, achieved by progressing through his sentence plan, he would be unlikely to get parole and was likely to remain longer in prison as a result. Catch 22.

It's been a nightmare. Basically I don't know what the rules and regulations are.

Three prisoners mentioned suicide or self harm:

When I first came in I was petrified The first one and a half years were really bad; I tried to commit suicide three times. Learning disabilities (healthcare)

They know I haven't self harmed for two years but they (prison officers) watch me every now and again. Woman prisoner

Good things about being in prison

Smaller numbers of prisoners, fewer than one in ten, had more positive things to say about being in prison:

Being here has helped me with my reading and writing as I do Toe-by-Toe[17] and go to a reading class on a Wednesday.
Scotland, possible learning disabilities

It's done me good coming to prison; it's made me a different person. It's made me more mature, think more and listen to people's views. It's made me a different person. It's probably made me a better person. I wasn't bad before.
Young offender, possible learning disabilities

This last sentence I learnt a lot about myself and other people that I didn't know. It gave me an open mind. I don't want to get back into this situation.

One prisoner was able to give a 'then and now' comparison:

I was in prison at 18 years old for robbery. I am now in my 40s and prison has improved. The toilets used to be buckets, the food can be alright sometimes, but it used to be awful. Now you can get education and you can use the phones and work — I work in the tailors. It stops you cracking in your cell. I have a TV here too. It's also cleaner and they check for drugs, which is good. You can also get help with your reading and writing. I have learnt to read in here.

Did prisoners understand why they were in prison?

Apart from two, everyone said they understood why they were in prison.

Did prisoners know when their release or parole date was?

Prisoners were asked if they knew when they could go home. Just under a fifth of prisoners didn't know because they were either on remand or had indeterminate sentences[18]. Discounting this group around one in ten said they didn't know when they could go home. This more than doubled for those with possible learning or borderline learning disabilities, almost a quarter of whom said they did not know when they could go home.

Sentence plans

Prisoners in England and Wales serving 12 months and more, and young prisoners sentenced when they were 18-20 years of age with at least four weeks left to serve, should have a sentence plan. A sentence plan is an important document for prisoners in that it details interventions, for example offending behaviour programmes that an offender must complete in order to progress through his sentence; good progression has a direct bearing on parole and release dates.

There are similar arrangements for prisoners in Scotland, the main difference being that all prisoners should have a sentence or community integration plan (this will be referred to as a sentence plan throughout the report).

This section on sentence plans includes prisoners serving sentences of 12 months or more in England and Wales and all prisoners in Scotland.

Did prisoners know what a sentence plan was for?

Prisoners were asked if they knew what a sentence plan was for and most said they did and were mostly correct in their understanding; those with possible learning and borderline learning disabilities were slightly less likely to be correct in their understanding than other prisoners.

---

[17] Run by the Shannon Trust, Toe-by-Toe is a literacy scheme that works with prisons to develop teams of prisoners who are able to read who act as mentors for those prisoners who cannot; the scheme is supported by the Prison Officers Association and prison officers are often involved in organizing Toe-by-Toe in local prisons

[18] An indeterminate public protection sentence (IPP) is, in effect, a life sentence and it contains three elements: a 'tariff' that is a period of imprisonment judged to be a just desert for the crime committed; an unlimited time of detention until the prisoner can prove he is no longer a threat to the public, and release under license (PRT briefing, Indefinitely Maybe?, 2007).

Did prisoners have a sentence plan?

Less than half of prisoners said they had a sentence plan. Prisoners with possible learning and borderline learning disabilities were the least likely to say they had a sentence plan and the comparison group were the most likely.

Of those who said they did have a sentence plan, prisoners with possible learning and borderline learning disabilities were the least likely to say they had a copy and the comparison group were the most likely to have a copy.

Most prisoners who said they had a sentence plan said they knew what was in it.

Daily living

This section looks at the daily living experiences of prisoners, for example how generally they got along in prison and what they did during the day; it includes:

1. reading prison information and filling in prison forms
2. support with 'daily living'
3. understanding what was going on and being understood
4. friends in prison
5. activities, including work in prison, education and library visits
6. time spent alone
7. sharing a cell
8. feeling unwell
9. being scared and being bullied
10. staying in touch with family and friends.

1. Reading prison information and filling in prison forms

Information for prisoners is generally made available in written form, for example leaflets and books, on notice boards and 'posted' under cell doors. Prisoners must complete application forms or 'apps' for their meals, their 'canteen' (prison shop), to request visits from family and friends, to make a complaint and in some prisons to make an appointment to see healthcare and to get their laundry done.

Prisoners were asked whether they had any difficulties reading prison information and filling in forms. This section looks first at reading prison information and then at filling in prison forms. Some common themes are reported at the end of both sections, which are:

• difficulties experienced asking for help
• pride at having improved literacy skills while in prison.

Reading prison information

```
Everything is written for a very educated
person and the words are very long. It's
really a humiliation if you have to ask
someone.
```

Prisoners were asked whether they had any difficulties reading prison information and 69% said they did, which rose to 85% for those with possible learning disabilities. None of the comparison group said they experienced difficulties reading prison information. This finding was highly statistically significant ($p < 0.001$).

Prisoners who said they had difficulties reading prison information were asked what happened. While most said they asked for and generally received help, a significant minority felt unable to ask for help or chose not to. For a number of prisoners whether they asked for help or not varied, sometimes they did and on other occasions they did not. Overall:

• 75% of prisoners who said they had difficulty reading prison information asked for, or sometimes asked for, and received help, which fell to 61% for prisoners with possible learning and borderline learning disabilities
• 38% of prisoners who said they had difficulty reading prison information said they didn't, or sometimes didn't, read prison information, which rose to 46% for prisoners with possible learning and borderline learning disabilities.

Asking for help

Most prisoners who said they needed help generally asked for and received help. An analysis of qualitative data showed that help asked for might involve help with reading information, help with understanding what the information means, or both. For most prisoners in this group asking for help was straight forward:

```
If something comes through the door I
will just bang on the wall and ask the
girl who lives in the next cell what it's
about. She's a Toe-by-Toe mentor, so it's
great.
```

It's not the reading that's the problem;
it's understanding what it's about. I
will ask anyone for help.

Help was sought from a variety of different people.
Slightly more prisoners said they would ask a member
of prison staff rather than another inmate. Prison staff
who were asked for help included, wing or landing
officers, personal and other prison officers, and
education staff; one prisoner said he would ask
healthcare and another, in Scotland, his speech and
language therapist. A number of prisoners qualified
which staff they would ask, which they would not and
why:

I will sometimes ask my personal officer
for help If I ask the others they will
take the piss and try to ignore you.
Young offender

The tutors in education would help, we
feel comfortable with them, not the
officers.

It depends on the officer. Don't get me
wrong, you get some officers who don't
care and others will help. It depends on
which officer it is. All prisons are the
same. Young offender

Several prisoners noted how busy officers seemed so
that even if they felt able to ask for help, it wasn't
always forthcoming:

If you ask the officers for help, they
say they will come back later but they
don't. Young offender with possible learning disabilities

I just have to wait for the right officer
to come along. 70% say 'yes, I'll come
later' but they don't and then it's lock
up and by then it's too late. Some
officers will help you there and then, or
come back to you within five minutes.
Young offender

Prisoners who asked for help from other inmates were
more likely to ask those who were also friends, cell
mates or family members, but this strategy wasn't
always successful:

They put something under the door, I
might ask my cousin, he's not much better
and he might say, 'oh, that's rubbish,
don't worry about it' and then I don't
know what it said.

Smaller numbers asked for help from inmates who
they identified as being the most able, including
library and induction orderlies, Samaritan Listeners
and Toe-by-Toe mentors:

I go to another prisoner called John in
the library and he helps me to read it
and explains it to me. Even when I do
read things myself I don't always
understand it.

A small number of prisoners said they would ask
'anyone'.

Not reading prison information
Prisoners who said they didn't or sometimes didn't
read prison information were asked what happened
and almost a quarter said that for them it meant not
knowing what was happening:

Then I don't know what's going on. Nobody
helps. Prisoner with possible learning disabilities

I have a problem reading signs as they
will put a sign up if there is a concert
in the gaol, but they won't tell people.
Scotland, possible learning disabilities

**I take a guess, or I just get
on the best I can. I just do
whatever. They got me to
sign something the other
day, I didn't know what it
said, I just signed it.** Young offender

Some prisoners explained that they had missed out on certain things as a result of not being able to read prison information:

I end up not knowing what it's about and that has happened to me before. I ended up with no credits on my phone once.
Woman prisoner

Others described feelings of frustration and anger:

If I don't read it I wouldn't know what's going on. Usually I just kick off and then I get into trouble. Woman prisoner

If I don't read it, I'm stuck and it's horrible. Woman prisoner

If I can't read it I just get angry.

Just under a fifth described how they tried their best to read prison information, sometimes they felt they got the 'gist' of it and other times not:

I try and do it myself, I may be a bit slow but I manage to do it.
Possible borderline learning disabilities

I can read some things but not others. I skim over the words that I don't know and then it doesn't make sense to me. I thought this interview was about learning to read. Young offender possible learning disabilities

Filling in prison forms

It's nearly all forms: going to the doctors, asking for something — you have to fill in a form.

The forms are so long winded, it's a big sheet. I think they make them a bit scary, it's very formal and they don't need to be so bad, and then you have to pluck up courage to ask for help and you feel inadequate and show weakness.

Prisoners were asked if they had difficulties filling in prison forms and 69% said they did, which rose to 78% for prisoners with possible learning disabilities. One of the comparison group said they had difficulties filling in prison forms. This finding was highly statistically significant (p < .0.001).

Prisoners who said they had difficulties filling in prison forms were asked what happened. While most said they asked for and generally received help, a significant minority felt unable to ask for help or chose not to. For a number of prisoners whether they asked for help or not varied, sometimes they did and on other occasions they did not. Overall:

- 82% of prisoners said they asked for or sometimes asked for and received help filling in prison forms, which rose to 88% for prisoners with possible learning and borderline learning disabilities
- 23% of prisoners said they didn't or sometimes didn't fill in prison forms, which fell to 16% for prisoners with possible learning and borderline learning disabilities.

Asking for help

The pattern of help asked for by prisoners for filling in prison forms was similar to that as for reading prison information, although only a very small number of prisoners said they also needed help with understanding what the form was about.

Help for filling in prison forms was asked for and received from a variety of different people. Prisoners were marginally more likely to ask for help from prison staff than they were from other inmates. Once again a number of prisoners qualified which staff they would ask, which they would not and why:

Some of the guards will help you, if they are not busy and if I ask politely. Some of the screws just can't be bothered in this prison. Possible borderline learning disabilities

I ask my personal officer for help, if he wasn't there it would be difficult to get help. Young offender

A male nurse helped me with the 'no smoking' course application. I don't really fill in forms but someone helps me if I need them to, but mostly I don't fill in any.

A very small number said that sometimes staff noticed they needed help filling in forms and so they didn't always have to ask:

The staff (prison officers) sometimes notice that I need help so I don't always have to ask. Young offender

As for reading prison information, several prisoners noted how busy officers seemed to be so that even if they felt able to ask for help filling in prison forms, it wasn't always forthcoming. It wasn't always prison officers who were 'too busy':

There are quite a few lads on the wing and they give you a hand. I always try to find someone or you don't get anything. It's embarrassing really. Sometimes they say, 'oh, leave it and I'll do it later' and then I have to wait for them.

Prisoners who asked for help filling in prison forms from other inmates were most likely to ask those who were also friends, cell mates or family members, with fewer relying on more able inmates as they did for reading prison information:

Other inmates will do them for me in the mornings if I need help. One does my canteen sheets for me and the other does my menus. Woman prisoner

If I can't fill in the forms I will get my cell mate to write it out for me, just so I don't have to go to the office. We all have a bit of trouble but we manage between us. Possible learning disabilities

I push it through the piping into the cell next door and they sometimes fill it in for me.
Young offender, possible learning disabilities

Small numbers said they would ask 'anyone'.

Not filling in prison forms

Prisoners who said they didn't or sometimes didn't fill in prison forms were asked what happened and over a third said that for them it meant not getting the things they wanted, getting the wrong things and missing out on things:

I don't fill in any applications, I don't get anything. Nobody helps me. I get embarrassed asking for help so I don't ask, there's no point. Woman prisoner

Once I didn't get to go to the gym because I couldn't fill in the form and at the time I couldn't find anyone to help. Possible learning disabilities

You get a meal sheet but it comes through the door. You have to hand it in before you get out of your cell and loads of the meals I get aren't what I want. Everything is one big problem.
Possible borderline learning disabilities

I couldn't fill in the visiting forms when I first came so I missed visits, then I was told what to do and somebody filled it in for me. Young offender

The things I can't fill in I just leave them out. Sometimes wrong things get delivered so I stay away from important things.

One prisoner didn't realize he had a difficulty with filling in forms until nothing happened as a result:

I had no problems with the visiting forms in the first week, I handed them in and everything but I wasn't getting visits, so I asked the guy on the hall what I was doing wrong and then I got the visits.
Scotland

A number of prisoners expressed anger about the difficulties they experienced with prison forms:

That's my sort of hell, filling in forms. It sends my temper through the roof; if I can't fill it in it does my head in.
Young offender

I couldn't fill in the visiting forms when I first came so I missed visits, then I was told what to do and somebody filled it in for me. Young offender

I can't understand some of the forms, or
there are words that I don't know and I
just get mad again. Woman prisoner

One prisoner said he had been in trouble for not filling
in prison forms:

If I don't fill in forms I get into
trouble, I have got adjudication before.

A number described how they tried their best to fill in
prison forms:

I do my best, but then people might think
it's a childish application because I
can't do it very well. I don't ask
anyone. Possible learning disabilities

I try to fill it in and then I ask staff
to check it and if they are decent staff
they will check it for me.
Learning disabilities (healthcare)

Some people can think in their head what
they want to say, or they can say it, but
then you can't put the same thing down on
paper and it's frustrating. I have always
had trouble with my full stops and
putting them in the right place and my
spelling isn't good.

Common themes concerning reading prison information and filling in forms

· Difficulties experienced in asking for help with
  reading information and filling in forms

A number of prisoners found asking for help difficult:
slightly less than a fifth said they found it difficult
asking for help to read prison information, with
smaller numbers finding it difficult asking for help to
fill in prison forms. Reasons given included not
knowing who to ask, a lack of confidence, fear of
ridicule, feelings of shame and embarrassment at not
being able to read and write and not wanting to
bother other inmates who may have their own
problems to deal with.

Nobody tells you who can help, you've got
to find out and because I can't read or
write I can't ask anyone and nobody
comes.

I generally try and ask my friend but for
one, I feel I am pressuring him because
he's got his own problems.

If somebody doesn't help me I'm stuck.
It's hard work and if it's confidential
you don't want people to know but you've
still got to ask.

One prisoner said she didn't ask for help because:
we were told not to rely on other people.

Asking staff for help, in particular from prison officers
was not an option that everyone felt comfortable
with:

I don't ask an officer because I don't
know what he will say and he might tell
everyone. Possible learning disabilities

I don't ask the officers because they
just talk about all of us and I don't
want them talking about my business. They
just laugh at you. I told one once that I
didn't go to education because I couldn't
read, write or spell and I was
embarrassed. He thought I was joking.
Woman prisoner

A number of prisoners felt that prison officers didn't
take their requests for help seriously enough or didn't
believe that the prisoner actually needed help:

The staff won't help, they say to me that
it should be in my words rather than
theirs, or sometimes they just can't be
bothered to help.
Scotland, possible learning disabilities

I do ask for help Jenny, but sometimes
they won't do it for you. They say, 'I've
read your letters, you don't need help.'
But Jenny, I can't always read things and
I do need help. Young offender

· Improved literacy skills
A small number of prisoners, around one in ten, were
proud of having improved their literacy skills while in
prison, which helped with reading information and
filling in forms:

I did have difficulties when I first came
in and now I'm on that adult literacy and
it's wicked! I've got my, what's it
called, my exams in English. When I first
came in I couldn't read but now when I'm
in the library I'm always looking at the
books. Young offender

I can do my menu and my canteen sheet now
but when I first came in I couldn't on
laundry day I get the cell next door to
write it down for me if the stuff goes
missing you don't get it back if it's not
written down. Young offender

2. Support with 'daily living'

As well as help with reading prison information and filling in forms, prisoners were asked what other help they received, including choosing meals, reading and writing letters, telling the time, getting clothes cleaned, making telephone calls and arranging visits. Half said they received help with some of the above and one of the comparison group. Prisoners with possible learning or borderline learning disabilities were the most likely to say they received help. A small number of prisoners said they didn't know who they could ask for help or what help they could ask for and so didn't ask anyone:

I don't get anything offered and I never
ask. Possible borderline learning disabilities

Because I can't read I don't know what I
can ask for. Even if you do find
somebody, they don't ever give you a
straight answer.

I don't really speak to anyone so I don't
ask for help I just stay in my pad.
Young offender

Others had developed their own way of coping:

Do you know how I cope? I laugh, I have
learnt to laugh. That gives you
pheromones. Learning disabilities (healthcare)

I have my way of dealing with it myself;
I may do it badly but I get by.
Young offender

Help with choosing meals

Around one in five said they got help filling in their menu sheets, which rose to one in three for prisoners with possible learning or borderline learning disabilities. Most who received help said it came from other prisoners. Some however did not receive help:

Before my brother came I just used to
tick it and hope for the best. I knew 'a'
was sandwiches, so I lived off
sandwiches. The officers won't fill your
menus out, they say just ask a prisoner.
Possible learning disabilities

I eat the same thing every time; I manage
by copying from the previous form.

I see the name of the food but I don't
know what is says, so I will go for
something that I know and like and that's
normally chips or sandwiches.

Help with reading and writing letters

One in four said they got help reading and writing letters, which rose to more than one in three for prisoners with possible learning or borderline learning disabilities. Help was most likely to come from other prisoners.

Help with arranging visits from family and friends[19]

Smaller numbers, fewer than one in ten, said they got help with arranging visits from family and friends, which rose to one in five for prisoners with possible learning or borderline learning disabilities. A number said they had learnt how to fill in visiting forms or managed by copying from previously completed forms, and no longer required help.

Help with cleaning clothes

Smaller numbers, fewer than one in ten, said they got help with laundry, which was most likely to come from another prisoner. In some prisons there were forms to be filled in and at others not. Some prisoners did their own laundry to avoid having to fill in forms.

Help with telling the time

Four prisoners said they got help with telling the time, one of whom had possible learning disabilities. However an analysis of qualitative data suggested that at least 16 prisoners, around one in ten, had difficulties in telling the time.

---

19. See also PRT submission to the Joint Committee on Human Rights, The Human Rights of Adults with Learning Disabilities, call for evidence, June 2007

Not being able to tell the time had a knock on effect for some prisoners:

```
My friend helps me by letting me share
her slot. You normally have to book a
time on the washing machine but sometimes
I miss it because I can't tell the time.
```
Woman prisoner

Some were able to manage with particular types of clocks or watches but not with others. For example a number of prisoners said they could manage if the clock were digital or by using their own watch. One prisoner said:

```
I have only just learnt how to do this,
one officer helped me.
```
Young offender

One said that he had trouble with 24 hour clocks and therefore also with completing visiting forms:

```
I have trouble reading a 24 hour clock,
which is how the visiting forms are
written.
```

Help with making telephone calls

Four prisoners said they got help making phone calls, however an analysis of qualitative data suggested that at least 12 prisoners, slightly fewer than one in ten experienced some difficulties with making phone calls:

```
I don't know how to use the phone; it's
that PIN thing isn't it?
```
Woman prisoner

One prisoner explained that he had difficulties because of his hearing:

```
There's too much noise when I try to make
calls because I wear a hearing aid. I
need a mini-com.
```
Possible learning disabilities

Two commented on the high cost of phone calls[20]:

```
I use the phone all the time. Most of my
money goes on phone call. I think people
who can't read or write should get extra
money to make phone calls.
```

Somebody special to ask for help or to talk to

Prisoners were asked if there was somebody special who they could ask for help whenever they needed to or whatever their difficulty or concern was, and whether there was somebody special who they felt they could talk to or confide in whenever they needed to.

• Somebody special to ask for help

Over half said there was somebody special who they could ask for help; prisoners with possible learning or borderline learning disabilities were the least likely to say so. Those who said they didn't have somebody special to ask for help said:

```
It would be good to have someone like
that.
```
Woman prisoner

```
If there is, I don't know about it.
```

```
You have a safer custody officer and
mental health team and there are a few
counselling teams that has really helped
me. But it took six months of self harm
before I got it and I was on 24 hour
suicide watch. The trouble is self harm
is the norm in here, it doesn't ring
bells.
```

Of those who said there was somebody special, around four-fifths said it was a member of prison staff and most likely a prison officer. Some prisoners referred specifically to their personal or lifer officer and smaller numbers mentioned staff from the chaplaincy, healthcare, education and psychology:

```
I can talk to one of the officers  I call
him my gaol dad.
```
Scotland, young offender, possible learning disabilities

```
I speak to Mrs X, she is an officer on
our wing, I call her mum number two.
```

```
There is an officer on B3 who I can ask
for help, I can't fault him. What a guy!
He listens to you.
```
Young offender

Less than a quarter said their 'somebody special' to ask for help was another inmate who was often described as a friend or who was their cell mate.

---

20. In September 2008, following a 'super complaint' about the high cost of phone calls for prisoners, made by the National, Scottish and Welsh Consumer Councils with support from the Prison Reform Trust, Ofcom ruled that prisoners in state run jails were paying more to make telephone calls than were prisoners in contracted out (privately run) jails. Ofcom invited the Justice Ministries' to consider opening negotiations with BT (for England and Wales) and Siemens (for Scotland) to reduce the price of calls (silicon.com, 23 September 2008).

Although movement of prisoners (and staff) wasn't highlighted generally as a problem, the following quote demonstrates how important 'somebody special', once found, can be:

```
That was my first cell mate. I was really
begging the officer not to take him away
and move him. It's hard to ask people to
help as it might be the wrong time and it
might annoy them.  Possible learning disabilities
```

• Somebody special to talk to
Over half said there was somebody special who they could talk to. Some who said there wasn't anyone special to talk to said:

```
I just bottle things up, so I blow every
couple of months and get into trouble for
it.  Scotland, young offender
```

```
If I say I am feeling down all they do is
put me in a cell, the tear proof sort, I
only get help when I cut myself.
```
Scotland, possible learning disabilities

```
I don't generally talk to people about
stuff. If I get really worked up I may
punch the walls or scream into a pillow.
Sometimes I find myself curled up in a
corner and I don't know why. Scotland
```

Of those who said there was somebody special to talk to, prisoners were most likely to say it was a member of prison staff and most likely a prison officer, which rose slightly for those with possible learning or borderline learning disabilities. As for 'special help', above, some prisoners referred specifically to their personal or lifer officer and smaller numbers mentioned staff from the chaplaincy, healthcare, including in Scotland speech and language therapy staff, education and psychology.

Concern over the movement of 'somebody special' was raised again by a different prisoner:

```
My mate Keith and my personal officer are
good to talk to but they changed her to a
different wing.
```

Less than one in five said they were aware of Samaritan listeners who they could talk to:
```
There are listeners in here that people
can talk to. They are good people, but I
have never used them but I have heard
they are good.
```
Young offender, possible learning disabilities

```
I'm not sure what they are called but
there are people who come around and ask
if you're OK.
```
Woman prisoner, possible learning disabilities

Although most prisoners who mentioned Samaritan listeners were willing to talk to them, a number expressed concern about the listener being a fellow prisoner and possible lack of confidentiality

```
I have used the listeners before but
basically if you tell another prisoner
they just spread it about.  Young offender
```

3. Understanding what is happening in prison and being understood
Knowing what is going on or is expected of you, and being able to solicit and receive information are things that most people take for granted. In any large or busy institution it can take a while to 'get the hang of things'. In prison, knowing what is going on and what is expected of you is especially important – getting things wrong can have serious consequences, for example prison rules may be broken or requests not properly made.

Understanding what is happening
Prisoners were asked what they would do if they didn't understand something in prison. While most said they would ask somebody, others said they would do nothing, or that they didn't know what they would do. An analysis of qualitative data showed that:

• Slightly fewer than three quarters of prisoners said they would ask somebody, which fell to around a half for those with possible learning or borderline learning disabilities. Prisoners said they might ask another inmate or a member of staff with many qualifying their response by saying they felt comfortable asking some members of staff but not others. Everyone in the comparison group said they would ask somebody. One prisoner said that one of the officers sometimes anticipated her need for help in understanding:

One of the prison officers is aware of my learning difficulties and she always says to me, 'do you understand?' and if I don't she will say it another way. But some officers say, 'well I have told you once and I am not telling you again'.
Woman prisoner

One prisoner said he would pretend that he knew what was going on:

I would just act like I know what they are talking about basically, but then I would walk away wondering what they were talking about. Scotland

And another said he might ask:

I have got the voice to ask but if I was intimidated I wouldn't. Sometimes if you go to the officers they will swear at you and tell you to go away.

- Under a fifth said they would do nothing, which rose to over a quarter for prisoners with possible learning or borderline learning disabilities. There were no prisoners in the comparison group who said they would do nothing:

I wouldn't do anything really; I'd be too scared to ask, so I'd do nothing.
Scotland, possible learning disabilities

Fuck knows what I would do. I would just ignore it and hope it goes away.
Young offender, possible learning disabilities

- Four prisoners said they didn't know what they would do and three said they would get angry:

I get the hump and storm out.

I would kick off.
Young offender, possible learning disabilities

- One prisoner said he would panic and self harm, and showed the researcher marks and scars on his arms.

Being understood

Prisoners were asked if there had ever been times when they felt that others didn't understand what they were trying to say to them. Slightly fewer than three quarters said this had happened to them and under half of the comparison group; prisoners with possible learning disabilities were the most likely to say this had happened to them.

However an analysis of qualitative data suggests that it wasn't just about 'being understood'. While some clearly had difficulty in making themselves understood, for others it seemed more about prisoners feeling that what they were trying to convey, to officers in particular, was not believed or taken seriously; that officers did not always listen to them; that they received unhelpful responses from officers, and were not 'getting anywhere' with requests for information or concerns, including frustration with 'the system'.

Of those who said there had been times when they felt that people didn't understand what they were trying to say to them, an analysis of qualitative data showed that:

- Over half said they had difficulties making themselves understood, which rose to more than two thirds for prisoners with possible learning or borderline learning disabilities. Reasons given by prisoners included words coming out in a muddle, not being able to pronounce certain words, using the wrong words, not being able to explain things properly, talking too fast, having a speech impediment, and for a small number having a strong regional accent. Only one in the comparison group said he had difficulties making himself understood which he put down to a strong Glaswegian accent.

That happens to me all the time. I muddle up words and that causes problems.
Scotland, young offender

I was always getting slagged off by other inmates on another hall about my hearing and my speech, but there are two other guys on my hall that can use sign language.
Scotland, young offender, possible learning disabilities

They (prison officers) always say to me, 'what?' And when I say it again they just call me stupid because I can't say the words properly. Woman prisoner

That happens most of the time; I get depressed when people don't understand me so I leave them alone, but then it doesn't get done. They say I don't explain properly, well if they gave me more time I would. Woman prisoner

Some said they had learned to persevere in order to make themselves understood:

I just need to explain things again and again. Scotland, possible learning disabilities

That has happened plenty of times, but eventually I keep going and they understand.

Three prisoners said they just wouldn't bother if they were not understood and two said they got angry:

I get the hump and walk out. I get angry but I don't start violence.

- Just under a quarter related not being understood to a perception that what they were trying to say was not believed by officers or taken seriously, and officers not listening to them.

It happened yesterday with one of the screws. I'm supposed to get a diabetic night pack but I was given one with a higher dose than the other boy on the wing, but the officer wasn't listening to me. I told him I should be on a lower dose. I just left it, walked away, there's no point arguing. Young offender

It has happened loads, like down at education, she gave me some work and I said I couldn't do it and she said to me, 'yes you can', I said I couldn't and because of that she gave me a written warning and kicked me out.
Young offender, possible learning disabilities

- Under a fifth related not being understood to receiving unhelpful responses, from officers in particular, not 'getting anywhere' with requests for

information or concerns, including frustration with 'the system'. Over a half of the comparison group felt this way.

It's like now, like when I'm trying to say I can't learn no more. I have been to a special school and I have learnt as much as I can, but they don't believe that. But why should I be punished for two things? I'm being punished for the crime and again for not being able to read and write[21].

I have been trying to get on education because what's the point me being in a workshop with all these signs and all this equipment when I can't read the notices? 'Oh, you'll be OK sweeping up', that was their answer. It's hard to get on education now. Possible learning disabilities

With one of the officers it was about getting my clothes when I first came here. I didn't know there was a 28 day limit to get your clothes in. A friend came to bring my clothes but they said he couldn't because 28 days had passed. I told the prison officer that I didn't know and he said to me, 'don't you read the rule book?' I would have done if I was given one. The prison officer couldn't understand that I didn't know about the 28 day rule. Comparison group

4. Friends in prison
Most prisoners said they had friends in prison; the comparison group were most likely to say so.

5. Activities in prison
Work:
Prisoners were asked if they had a job in prison and 61% said they had. However this reduced to 41% for prisoners with possible learning or borderline learning disabilities and for prisoners with possible low average IQ the rate was even lower at 38%.

Library visits:
Over half of prisoners said they visited the library which reduced slightly for those with possible learning or borderline learning disabilities.

21.   This prisoner was serving an IPP sentence.

Most prisoners who didn't visit the library said it was because they couldn't read very well or lacked confidence or because they felt there was nothing there for them:

```
I don't go because I can't read. I used
to get stories on CDs but they never
change them, they are all the same.
```
Possible learning disabilities

A small number of prisoners said they didn't visit the library because they hadn't been asked or had never been shown where it was. Two prisoners from one prison said they were unable to go to the library because it clashed with their time at education; one said that he was unable to visit the library because he was 'on basic'[22] and at one prison three prisoners said they didn't go to the library because the library 'comes to us'.[23]

Prisoners who visited the library went for a variety of reasons, including Toe-by-Toe, to look at magazines and pictures, borrow CDs, read newspapers, to practice 'theory' for ECDL (European Computer Driving Licence), to meet friends, take part in 'library groups' and to borrow books:

```
I go on Fridays. I can read books now,
even though it takes me a long time. My
first book took me nearly a year and a
half to read.
```
Learning disabilities (healthcare)

```
I went last week and I picked some books
with big writing. I took five.
```
Possible learning disabilities

> **I do go to the library, it's pretty good, but there aren't many books for people with dyslexia. There should be more to help people who struggle like I do.**
> **Woman prisoner**

Education:
Prisoners were asked if they were attending education classes and over half said they were. Prisoners with possible learning or borderline disabilities were the most likely group to be attending classes[24].

Although prisoners were not asked to say what they thought about the education classes they attended some were keen to explain:

```
I go for reading and writing; I've been
trying for ten years.
```
Scotland, woman prisoner, possible learning disabilities

```
I do go to education Jenny, yes. The
ladies from education teach me a lot: all
my spellings, full stops, capital
letters. I never went to education, I am
a traveller - but I can lay drives.
```
Young offender

```
I have done a diploma in IT, which is
good because before I came here I
couldn't even switch on a computer.
```
Woman prisoner

A number of reasons were given for not attending education, including:
• being on a waiting list
• a lack of suitable courses:

```
I feel the classes are not serving their
purpose. There should be more hands on
courses to expand our knowledge. They
send you out the same as you come in.
```

• being engaged in full time employment elsewhere in the prison
• never having been asked:

```
I haven't been asked if I want to go to
education, I don't mind going No one has
ever talked to me or assessed me for my
abilities to do activities.
```
Young offender, possible learning disabilities

• having been taken off education:
  - for unacceptable behaviour, which at one particular prison seemed a high proportion of the young prisoners interviewed:

---

22. Entitlements under the basic regime differ slightly from prison to prison, but basic status generally means a minimum level of privileges
23. Some prison libraries take the library service, or elements of it, to prisoners on the wings or landings
24. The high numbers of prisoners with possible learning or borderline learning disabilities attending education may reflect how prisoners were identified, which was largely through education staff.

The man won't let me go; he won't let me in there. He said to me that he doesn't want me fucking about. Young offender

I did go for two to three weeks but I was hyperactive and messing around too much so I don't go anymore. Young offender

- and for one prisoner, because she was unable to read:

I was in a classroom but because of my reading they moved me out to do Toe by Toe and then I can go back when I can read. Woman prisoner

• negative previous experiences of education or of prison education:

I can't do it. I get really, really angry. The writing books look different to me, I can't read it. I went to a special school; the teachers didn't listen to me. I assaulted a teacher when I was there and I went mad in that place. Young offender

I have tried but I don't like it as you get different teachers and not one on one help. The time between classes is also too long; I forgot everything in a week. Woman prisoner

• anxiety about being with other people, although a number of prisoners talked about having in-cell education:

I don't go because I just can't handle groups.

I used to go to education but I stopped because of panic attacks. Scotland

6. Time spent alone

Prisoners were asked how much time, on average, they spent on their own during the day and many spent long periods alone. Prisoners with possible learning or borderline learning disabilities were the most likely to spend the most time alone during the day with just under a third saying they spent between

one and six hours alone, see table 4. Most prisoners said they were in their cell when they were alone.

Table 4: time spent alone by prisoners:

	Comparison group %	Target group %	Possible LD or BLD %
Less than an hour	41	23	12
1-3 hours	18	28	19
1-6 hours	18	23	31
Varies	23	23	31
Don't know	0	3	7

All except four[25] prisoners had a television in their cell and most had radios and music systems, which were often combined systems.

Prisoners were asked what they did when they were on their own and they described a wide range of different activities including:

• watching television
• listening to music and for three prisoners playing music
• listening to the radio
• reading books, newspapers and magazines
• art, drawing, colouring, embroidery, sewing and model making
• writing, including letters, poetry, filling in forms and for one prisoner, a diary
• study, including use of a computer
• keep fit and exercise, including yoga
• playing games, including on a games console and doing puzzles
• praying and going to church
• keeping their cell clean and tidy
• sleeping
• 'nothing'
• thinking and worrying
• taking drugs
• smoking.

The most frequently mentioned activities were, in order, watching television, reading, writing letters, listening to music and sleeping in equal place, and art, including drawing, colouring, model making, sewing and embroidery.

---

25. The removal of televisions from prisoners' cells is often used as a punishment for certain behaviour and is part of being on a 'basic regime'.

Some prisoners mentioned only one activity while others listed a number and range of different activities. More than three quarters of the comparison group described two or more 'constructive' activities from the above list compared to less than half of those with possible learning or borderline learning disabilities.

What follows is how some prisoners described how they spent their time when they were on their own:

I watch TV, drink tea or sleep. There's not much I can do.
Scotland, possible learning disabilities

I just sleep when I'm by myself.
Woman prisoner, possible learning disabilities

I sleep. They're taking my television because of what happened in education[26].
Young offender, possible learning disabilities

I just sit there. I don't like TV. Young offender, possible learning disabilities

I started making models of matchsticks. I have made a camper van and a motor bike so far.

I write letters, I do puzzles in magazines, I knit for the shoe box appeal, I do cross stitch and I may watch TV and do a bit of yoga. Woman prisoner

Sometimes I watch TV and sometimes I write a letter to my kids; it takes forever but I do it.

I read, I do some work for my NVQ, I listen to music or I watch TV.
Woman prisoner, comparison group

I study and I write letters. I also try and pamper myself if I've got the things to do a facial or my feet or hands.
Woman prisoner, comparison group

7. Sharing a cell

Prisoners do not choose to share a cell or to be accommodated on their own; in overcrowded prisons single cell accommodation is often at a premium. A risk assessment determines the allocation of shared or single accommodation and a number of factors are taken into consideration.

In this study, prisoners with learning disabilities or difficulties were more likely to be allocated single cell accommodation than those in the comparison group, 73% and 53% respectively.

8. Feeling unwell

Prisoners were asked what they would do if they felt unwell. An analysis of qualitative data showed that:

- While most prisoners said they knew what they would do if they felt unwell, fewer than two-thirds of those with possible learning or borderline learning disabilities said they did. Prisoners variously said they would go to healthcare, see the nurse or the doctor, fill in a form, press the cell buzzer and tell a member of staff.

- Slightly fewer than one in five prisoners with possible learning or borderline learning disabilities said they would need help to access healthcare and were the most likely to say so.

I know you have to fill in a form but I wouldn't know what to put on it. Scotland, woman prisoner, possible learning disabilities

I would have to get somebody to fill in a form, you shouldn't have to do that, you should be able to go down and just say so. You should be able to phone them like on the outside.

- Around one in ten said they would do nothing, for a number of reasons. Some because they preferred to manage minor complaints themselves and some because they didn't think healthcare was very good. One prisoner said he would do nothing because it meant filling in a form.

- Smaller numbers said they didn't know what they would do. Prisoners with possible learning or borderline learning disabilities were the most likely to say they didn't know, more than one in ten. There were no prisoners in the comparison group who said they didn't know what they would do if they felt unwell.

Although prisoners were not asked what they thought about healthcare or what happened when they felt unwell many were keen to explain:

26. The prisoner had been taken off education for disruptive behaviour and put onto a 'basic regime'.

I don't know, I haven't been feeling well for the past couple of days but I haven't done anything about it because it means filling in another form. Scotland

I see healthcare every two weeks, one to have a good chinwag and secondly to have my blood pressure checked and my weight. I have a CPN nurse who I go to and talk as well. Learning disabilites (healthcare)

You have to put an application in to see the doctor if you're sick but that's a nightmare. I keep asking the doctor to review my medication and my psychiatrist because I can't sleep, but I can't get anywhere. Possible learning disabilities

You have got to wait to see a nurse and sometimes they don't even put your name down. I wanted to see a nurse and he (the officer) said what for and I wouldn't tell him, I didn't think he should know, so just because I wouldn't tell him he wouldn't let me go.
Young offender, possible learning disabilities

A number talked about how long it took to get an appointment with healthcare:

I would go to healthcare but it's pretty bad because you have to put in applications and by the time they see you, you're better.
Possible borderline learning disabilities

I had a broken finger and it took them five weeks to send me to hospital to have an x-ray. I have a lump under my arm and I am waiting to go and have an operation. It's a bit worrying because my mum and nan had cancer. I've been waiting a year here and also in x prison. At least here I did get to see a specialist.
Woman prisoner, comparison group

Two prisoners from the same prison told of the electricity being turned off in their cells if they had a 'rest day' due to sickness:

I would go and get some paracetomol off the nurse because if you are ill you get your electricity turned off, so it's like you are being punished for being ill.
Woman prisoner, comparison group

Another from the same prison said she would be too scared to report as sick:

I would go to work because I would be too scared about getting into trouble. That happens here, I daren't not go to work.
Woman prisoner

Although not directly a healthcare issue, the following situation was nevertheless very distressing for the prisoner concerned:

It could be an hour after you have pressed the buzzer before they answer it. I suffer from incontinence sometimes through stress, once I had to sit on a wet bed all night because the staff didn't have facilities to open the door (sic.)[27]. Scotland

9. Being scared and being bullied

Prisoners were asked whether they had been scared while in prison, whether they had been bullied or if anybody had ever been nasty to them, and what they would do if anything 'bad' happened to them in prison.

Had prisoners been scared in prison?

Over half of prisoners said they had been scared in prison. Prisoners with possible learning or borderline learning disabilities were the least likely to say they had been scared and one said he didn't know.

Those who said they had been scared were asked what happened. Prisoners said they had been scared for many different reasons including not understanding what was happening to them or what was expected of them, arriving into prison for the first time, being bullied and assaulted by other inmates and staff, and because they had been assaulted in the past and were scared it would happen again. Two prisoners said they were scared because they had been raped while in prison.

I have been scared through bullying, I can hear people planning things and talking about it, although it doesn't necessarily happen. I am scared in the shower, there are no cameras and no officers so if you are going to get done, that's where it will happen. I have seen this happen. Scotland, possible learning disabilities

```
I have been scared especially where I am
now, there's too much going on. You feel
a bit scared, there is fighting and
stabbing and there's hot oil attacks. You
can't turn your back on anyone; you can't
turn your back.

I hate seeing fights; I always run to my
room and lock the door.
```
Scotland, woman prisoner, possible learning disabilities

```
He (an officer) just started taking all my
stuff out, throwing it around and I
shouted at him to stop. He came at me,
grabbed me, twisted me up. I did nothing;
that incident actually shook me up.
```
Young offender

```
I am a bit scared in the shower someone
got raped in the shower by eight lads and
then two days later he killed himself and
that scared me. So now I feel nervous in
the shower.
```

Had prisoners ever been bullied, or had people been nasty to them?

Almost half said they had been bullied; prisoners with possible learning or borderline learning disabilities were least likely to say they had been bullied or that somebody had been nasty to them. No prisoners in the comparison group said they had been bullied.

The 'shower' was a common cause for concern amongst prisoners; it was where many felt the most vulnerable.

As well as describing incidents where prisoners felt they had been bullied or where people had been nasty to them, some also said who had helped – sometimes other inmates and sometimes members of staff.

A number described how they retaliated against possible bullying by 'standing up for themselves' or 'getting' other prisoners before they were 'got' themselves. Sometimes staff intervened and other times not:

```
They do try and bully you, like pushing
you and trying to get to the pool table
first, but the screws have helped.
```
Young offender, possible learning disabilities

```
I have been spat on, tripped up, and I
have been called names, although I can
handle that one. Things have been hidden
in my bed, for example they wet my bed
knowing I can't change it until the next
day. There's a lot of homophobic abuse,
no one helps, they just laugh and think
it's funny. The staff have nicknames for
me too, like 'fanny boy'.
```
Scotland, possible learning disabilities

```
They tried to bully me, but I wasn't
having it. I flip easily when people are
calling me names like, 'retard' or
'nonce'... When people started banging on
my cell wall to annoy me my neighbour
told them off.
```
Young offender

```
I have had lots of bullying done to me, I
still get a lot. The others make fun of
me and some of the officers laugh along.
My personal officer helps when she's on,
but none of the others have really
bothered about it. The other staff just
say, 'go behind your door' but you don't
always want to be on your own because
that's when you get down (depressed) and
start self harming again.
```
Woman prisoner

What would prisoners do if something 'bad' happened to them?

Prisoners were asked what they would do if something 'bad' happened to them in prison. One prisoner with possible learning disabilities said:

```
The only bad thing for me is people not
acknowledging me and being ignored.
There's no knowing what's going on.
```

An analysis of qualitative data showed that prisoners would respond to something 'bad' happening to them in a variety of different ways including physical retaliation; talking to somebody about it; trying to sort the situation out themselves, and reporting the incident to an officer. Some said they would do nothing and others that they didn't know.

- Less than a third said they would talk to somebody or report the incident to a prison officer; prisoners with possible learning disabilities and difficulties were most likely to say this.

If you're bullied in here you can go to
one of the officers and say somebody's
bullying you and they'll look out for
you. Scotland, possible learning disabilities

Some prisoners highlighted the risks involved in taking
such an approach:

You can do it the 'legal' way, but people
talk and it can go against you.

· Around a third said that if something bad happened
to them they would retaliate, which generally
meant meeting aggression with aggression; two
prisoners in the comparison group said they would
respond in this way.

I would probably retaliate; if he had hit
me I would probably beat the shit out of
him. I have anger management problems so
I probably wouldn't be able to control
myself. Scotland, possible learning disabilities

If I got beat up I would probably give
them a good kicking. I can't cope with
mental torture, physical I can cope with.
A few days in healthcare and then I would
be right as rain. I would be shocked but
not worried. Learning disabilities (healthcare)

I would try and deal with it what I mean
by 'deal with it' is get in the showers
and sort it out. Young offender

I would smash them up It's easier to
sort it out yourself.
Young offender, possible learning disabilities

I would just attack them. There's no
chance of going to an officer you would
just get a worse time for that.
Scotland, young offender

Not everyone said they would retaliate by using
physical aggression:

I would fight for my case, pay the person
back, not necessarily with fists but I
would fight back. Scotland, young offender

One prisoner with possible learning disabilities said
she would bide her time:

I would get out of prison and wait for
them, and then I would bang them when
they're not expecting it.
Woman, possible learning disabilities

· Smaller numbers, around one in ten, said they
would try to resolve the situation 'appropriately',
without commenting further on what was meant
by 'appropriate'. Sometimes this approach had an
ominous ring to it:

I would take care of things myself first
if it was possible. It's an unspoken
rule. Scotland

And on other occasions prisoners who took matters
into their own hands would opt for a verbally
mediated or other non-aggressive solution. One
young offender took a particularly mature approach,
which sounded like a response he had recently learned:

I know how to deal with that stuff now, I
just have a laugh and a joke and I say,
'would you like to be bullied?' I would
probably sort it out myself.

· Almost a quarter said they didn't know what they
would do or that they would do nothing, which
reduced to less than a fifth for those with possible
learning or borderline learning disabilities. No
prisoners in the comparison group said this.

I don't know. I would probably just lock
myself behind the door and never get out
again.

I don't know because when things go wrong
that's when I self harm. I have cut
myself up really bad, and tried to hang
myself, put a bag over my head and tied
it. Woman prisoner

Prisoners who said they would do nothing generally
said so for two reasons: there was no point, nothing
would happen as a result, or the consequences of
doing 'something' were likely to be worse than doing
'nothing':

What could I do? You tell me. (The
interviewer suggested he could make a complaint) Then
I would be labeled a grass and a lot more
people would want to hurt you.

There's nothing you can do in here. If you go through the proper channels it gets worse and they end up shipping you out, so what can you do? Young offender

- Smaller numbers said they it had never happened to them and they didn't want to think about it or that they would try to 'walk away', forget about it, bottle it up and 'go into a shell'.

10. Staying in touch with family and friends

Visits

Prisoners were asked if they received visits from family and friends and around two-thirds of prisoners said they did. Prisoners with possible learning or borderline learning disabilities were the least likely to receive visits.

Letters and cards

Prisoners were asked if they received letters and cards from family and friends and over four-fifths of prisoners said they did. Prisoners with possible learning disabilities were the least likely to receive letters and cards, fewer than three-quarters.

Around four-fifths sent letters and cards to family and friends; prisoners with possible learning disabilities were the least likely to send letters and cards, fewer than three quarters.

Telephone calls

Prisoners were asked if they made telephone calls to family and friends and over four- fifths said they did. Prisoners with possible learning disabilities were the least likely to make phone calls, around two-thirds.

Making a complaint

There is a formal complaints procedure for prisoners should they wish to make a complaint against, for example, other prisoners, members of staff or prison conditions. The complaints procedure is confidential.

Complaints do need sorting out so that the person making the complaint doesn't suffer as a result of putting in a complaint. Woman prisoner, comparison group

Prisoners were asked what they would do if they wanted to make a complaint. An analysis of qualitative data showed that:

- Fewer than half of prisoners were aware of a complaints form and/or process, which reduced to a third for those with possible learning or borderline learning disabilities. Three quarters of the comparison group were aware. Some prisoners said what they thought about the complaints process and while two were impressed:

I would fill in a CP2 form; my friends help me do that, my pals. I have done this before and it's worked.
Scotland, woman prisoner, possible learning disabilities

- many more were less so:

I would fill out a complaints form, I need someone to help me do that and then I get an answer back, written down. It takes a long time for me to fill it in and then they write back saying I have filled in the wrong form and I have to start again I filled in a form once, serious stuff, an officer threatened me and a governor came to talk to me and nothing happened and then they said there were no records of it. Possible learning disabilities

A number of prisoners said they would need help to fill in a complaints form, which put them off and so they were less likely or unlikely to make a complaint:

I don't bother complaining, they just say fill in a form and I can't. Woman prisoner

Some highlighted perceived risks associated with putting in a complaint:

I would put in a bullying application and the person would be on bully watch and if they are found to be a bully they get put on bully basic. But the thing is, if they know they are being watched they are not going to be a bully and then you go to the governor and he says, 'who says what?' so they know it's you and you still get it. Young offender

I can't even fill in a complaints form, so I don't complain about anything.
Woman prisoner

- Almost one in five said they would speak to a member of staff if they wanted to make a complaint. Prisoners with possible learning or borderline learning disabilities were the most likely to pursue this option, almost one in three. Some prisoners however had concerns about how their verbal complaint would be received:

`Normally you would go to an officer, but I wouldn't because they might not listen to me.` Possible learning disabilities

- Around one in five of prisoners said they wouldn't complain; it wasn't an option they were willing to pursue. Some prisoners qualified their response saying they might complain about a member of staff but never against another inmate, while others said that complaints against members of staff resulted in making an already bad situation worse:

`You wouldn't complain even if you wanted to. You would have to make sure the screws move you to the vulnerable person unit before making a complaint otherwise your life would be 20 times harder.` Possible learning disabilities

`I wouldn't complain about anybody, you would be a grass if you did.` Young offender, possible learning disabilities

`I did complain, I ended up at x prison. I'm too scared to complain, where will I end up? In Dartmoor away from my family? If you think I am lying you can check.` (The interviewer asked why he thought she would think he was lying.) `Because everyone is on their side.` Young offender

Around one in ten prisoners said there was no point in making a complaint:

`I have complained in the past but nothing ever happens and the officers make your life a lot harder then.` Woman prisoner

Prison rules and discipline

Prison rules
Prison rules play a large part in determining how the prison is run; they include how prisoners and prison staff should conduct themselves and what prisoners may and may not do.

For England and Wales, Prison Service Order[28] (PSO) 0100, the Prison Rules 1999; the Young Offender Institution (Amendment) (No. 2) Rules 1999 apply, which was last updated in February 2004. For Scotland, The Prisons and Young Offender Institutions (Scotland) Rules 2006 apply.

Knowing about prison rules
Prisoners were asked how they knew about prison rules. Some said they knew about the rules through formal ways, for example during prison induction, from the prisoner information book (described variously as a rule book or prison book), from leaflets, information on notice boards and being told by officers. Others relied on informal ways, for example watching what others did, figuring it out for themselves, using common sense and picking things up as they went along. Smaller numbers said they learnt by their mistakes, only getting to know about a rule once they had broken it, and others said they didn't know what the rules were. An analysis of qualitative data showed that:

- Just over two fifths said they knew about prison rules through formal ways. Prisoners with possible learning or borderline learning disabilities were most likely to say they knew about prison rules because prison officers had told them. Over two thirds of the comparison group said they knew about prison rules through formal ways.

`The rules are displayed on our wing and on the doors of the shower. There is a list of them.` Young offender, possible learning disabilities

`There is a pamphlet in the hall; they also tell you in induction.` Possible learning disabilities

That's easy. You know the rules when you break the rules.

Although some prisoners said they knew about the availability of written information explaining prison rules or remembered being told about the rules during induction it didn't necessarily mean they knew what the rules were:

> They are in a leaflet, some bits are easy to read and some are rushed.
> Possible learning disabilities

> I asked for a rule book. The rule book is written anyway so you don't really understand it. Scotland, young offender

> They read the rules out when you first come onto the wing, but I didn't really understand them all, there was too much going on in my head to take it in.
> Woman prisoner

- Over a third said they relied on informal ways to know about prison rules. A small number of prisoners, including two in the comparison group, said this was the only way to know about the rules because there was no written information available:

> Sometimes people will tip you off, but they don't tell you much. You're constantly guessing what the rules are and trying not to break them. Woman prisoner

> I learn them from overhearing the screws. When you come in there is an induction but mostly you find them out for yourself. Possible borderline learning disabilities

One prisoner made a point of finding out about prison rules as he was moved around the prison estate:

> When you come on the wing you go straight to the office and they tell you.
> Learning disabilities (healthcare)

- Over a tenth, and slightly more for those with possible learning or borderline learning disabilities, said they knew about prison rules only after they had broken one, when it was too late. Two prisoners in the comparison group said they knew about prison rules in this way.

> They don't tell you, you just get a written warning and you get put on basic, no TV. Young offender, possible learning disabilities

> That's easy. You know the rules when you break the rules.

> I know them because I got put on report and they gave me a list of rules.
> Scotland, young offender

- Smaller numbers, fewer than one in ten, didn't know what the rules were; some qualified this by saying that if you couldn't read you didn't have much chance of finding out. One prisoner with possible learning disabilities guessed that he might find the rules on a computer.

Breaking prison rules

Prisoners were asked whether they had ever broken a prison rule and over a half said they had. Prisoners in the comparison group were the least likely to say they had broken a prison rule.

Prisoners were asked if they knew what would happen if somebody broke a prison rule. An analysis of qualitative data showed that:

- The majority of prisoners understood that some sort of punishment would follow, depending on how serious the rule breaking had been, but not necessarily what the punishment would be. Examples given were: going from 'enhanced' to 'basic'; having your TV taken away; getting a 'nicking' or a warning; going down 'the blocks'; being sent to see the governor; getting adjudication; having a 'red entry' written in the prisoners personal file; being put on report and getting a verbal warning. Three prisoners all of whom had possible learning disabilities, and two of whom were from the same prison, said that breaking a prison rule meant that the prisoner would be harmed:

> You get beat up if you break a rule, and get taken down to segregation.
> Possible learning disabilities

> They would get a kicking in a room.
> Scotland, young offender, possible learning disabilities

- Fewer than one in ten said they didn't know what would happen if somebody broke a prison rule, two of whom had possible learning disabilities and two were from the comparison group.

Adjudication (England and Wales) and Orderly Room (Scotland)

According to the Prison Discipline Manual for England and Wales, Prison Service Order[28] (PSO) 2000, issue date December 2005, 'an adjudication has two purposes:

- to help maintain order, control, discipline and a safe environment by investigating offences and punishing those responsible;
- to ensure that the use of authority in the establishment is lawful, reasonable and fair.'

The Scottish Prison Service does not publish an equivalent manual to guide disciplinary procedures. The wording of the Prisons and Young Prisoners Institutions (Scotland) Rules 2006 implies equivalent attention to issues of fairness, including discretion from the Governor to 'permit the prisoner to be represented at the inquiry', (para.116.7). The prisoner, however, must apply for such a facility.

Prisoners in England and Wales were asked if they knew what 'adjudication' meant, and in Scotland, if they knew what the orderly room was and what happened there. Two thirds of prisoners said they did know, and slightly fewer in the comparison group.

Prisoners who said they did know were asked to explain their understanding. Prisoners with learning disabilities or difficulties were more likely to be broadly correct in their understanding than those in the comparison group, 63% and 55% respectively. Prisoners with possible learning or borderline learning disabilities were slightly more likely than the target group overall to be 'broadly correct' in their understanding and prisoners in the 'low average' group were markedly more likely, over 83% of whom were broadly correct in their understanding.

Control and restraint

The term 'control and restraint' is used to describe the use of permitted force against prisoners.

For England and Wales, PSO 1600, Use of Force, details the circumstances in which force can be used and the framework for justifying the use of force. According to PSO 1600, 'Control and restraint techniques are used as a last resort in order to bring a violent or refractory prisoner under control. The techniques are applied for as short a time as possible.'

The Prison Rules in Scotland are similar; Prison Rule 93(2) states that, 'an officer dealing with a prisoner shall not use force unnecessarily and, when application of force to a prisoner is necessary, no more force than is necessary shall be used.'

Prisoners were asked if they had been subject to 'control and restraint' at their current prison. Prisoners with learning disabilities and difficulties were five times as likely to say they had been subject to 'control and restraint' as those in the comparison group, 25% and 5% respectively. However this result was not highly statistically significant (p = 0.050).

Prisoners in the 'low average' group were most likely to say they had been subject to control and restraint.

Segregation

The term 'segregation' is used to describe when prisoners are isolated from other prisoners and the remainder of the prison.

At the time of writing a full review of PSO 1700, Segregation (England and Wales) was taking place. Under Prison Rule 45 (YOI Rule 49), Good Order or Discipline, the purpose and reasons for segregation are described thus:

Prisoners are only segregated for reasons of Good Order or Discipline when there are reasonable grounds for believing that a prisoner's behaviour is likely to be so disruptive or cause disruption that keeping a prisoner on ordinary location is unsafe.

For Scotland, Prison Rule 94 governs the removal of prisoners from association and provides certain safeguards including the amount of time a prisoner may be 'removed' prior to 'the written authority of the Scottish Ministers' being obtained, and attention from a medical officer 'as soon as practicable'. Written authority is only required if a prisoner's removal is likely to be in excess of 72 hours.

---

28. 'Prison Service Orders are long-term mandatory instructions which are intended to last for an indefinite period' (HM Prison Service web site).

Prisoners were asked if they had spent time in the segregation unit at their current prison. Prisoners with learning disabilities or difficulties were more than three times as likely to say they had spent time in the segregation unit as those in the comparison group, 37% and 11% respectively.

Almost half of prisoners in the 'low average' group said they had spent time in the segregation unit, 48%, and were the group most likely to say so.

Table 5: different levels of rule breaking, adjudication, control and restraint and segregation:

	Comparison group %	Target group %	Possible LD or BLD %	Low average IQ %
Broken a prison rule	42	58	53	52
Understand adjudication	55	63	68	83
Subject to control and restraint	5	25	27	30
Spent time in segregation	11	37	36	48

Reducing re-offending

Cognitive behaviour treatment programmes aim to change the way prisoners think, to bring home the effect of their behaviour on themselves and others, and to encourage prisoners to learn positive techniques to avoid the situations that lead to offending (SEU, 2002).

Prisoners were asked if they had done any programmes or classes to help them stop offending, for example offending behaviour programmes. Just over a third of prisoners said they had which reduced to a fifth, for prisoners with possible learning or borderline learning disabilities[29]. Over half of the comparison group said they had done such programmes.

Prisoners who hadn't done any such programmes were asked if they would like help to stop offending:

I tried to do cognitive skills but I was told I couldn't be part of it because I couldn't read and write. I asked for one to one but they told me they couldn't do that. Scotland

Yes I would but I can't read and write; it's very embarrassing. You can't do the courses if you can't read and write. Woman prisoner

There is no SOTP (sex offender treatment programme) at this prison, but I'm waiting to hear back from the social worker on being able to do it on the outside, possibly one to one. Scotland, woman prisoner

They sent me round the country for courses but I kept getting knocked back because of my learning difficulties, which means I'm not suitable. I'm going from pillar to post.

29. See also PRT submission to the Joint Committee on Human Rights, The Human Rights of Adults with Learning Disabilities, call for evidence, June 2007

> I think I should try to work in some kind of routine, a proper nine to five kind of job. I have lots of time to think and that's what I think I should do.
>
> **Possible borderline learning disabilities**

The Future

This section looks at prisoners' aspirations for the future and concerns about leaving prison and includes:

• what prisoners would like to do when they leave prison, and who might help

• worries about leaving prison

• whether prisoners thought they might come back to prison.

What prisoners would like to do when they leave prison, and who might help

I would like to decorate my house and behave myself. Possible learning disabilities

I hope to go back to my council job and be good. Young offender possible learning disabilities

I need to get a house and find a nice little job; if I get a job that will help me stay out of trouble. I also need to look after my mum.
Young offender, possible learning disabilities

I would like supported accommodation, help with my self harming and work at my reading and writing skills. I would also like to see an alcohol counselor and a psychologist. Scotland, possible learning disabilities

Prisoners were asked about the sorts of things they would like to do when they left prison. An analysis of qualitative data showed that prisoners had a range of aspirations for when they left prison, including finding work or going to college; seeing family and friends and re-building relationships; sorting themselves out and 'doing better'; finding somewhere to live, and generally getting on with life. Smaller numbers said they didn't know what they would do and one said he expected he would go back to crime.

• Finding work and going to college

Around half of prisoners said they wanted to find work on leaving prison, and slightly under a third said they wanted to go to college. The types of work that prisoners talked about included teaching navigation or marine surveying, work in the building trades, catering, working with computers, library work, as a drugs and alcohol worker and running their own business. College courses aspired to included health and safety, food hygiene and in the building trade:

I have done a painting and decorating course, x was a good gaol and now I have an NVQ1 in painting and decorating. I would like to do that when I get out. I'm getting on now, I'm 34 years old and I have never had a job. Possible learning disabilities

When I get out I know exactly what I'll do. I'm going to buy a truck, I can't drive so my dada's workmen will drive for me, I'll do a leaflet, put an ad in the paper, a free phone number and I'll get into laying drives as a business.
Young offender

One prisoner said he would like to go college, but didn't hold out too much hope:

I want to go to college, but how can I do that? I have tried before but they won't have me. Young offender, possible borderline learning disabilities

51

• Family and friends

Around a third said they would like to spend more time with family and friends and several talked about the need to re-build relationships. This reduced to a fifth for prisoners with possible learning or borderline learning disabilities.

• Sorting themselves out, doing better and getting on with life

Over a quarter spoke variously about 'sorting themselves out' and getting on with life. For five prisoners this meant moving away from previous geographical areas and severing relationships with friends and family members.

I am going to go shopping with Stephen (boyfriend) and get on with my life. I'm also going to move out of Sheffield, but I'm not sure where I'm going to go.
Woman prisoner, possible learning disabilities

I would like to start my charity bike rides again. I've done 1,000 miles in eight days before, I like being outside, I'm very energetic.   Possible learning disabilities

I will have to start a new life. I would like to work on the lifeboat again if they let me back on. I would also like to start all my ambulance training again, if they let me, but it will be a struggle.

• Finding somewhere to live

Around one in ten, said they would need to find somewhere to live.

• Don't know'

Around one in ten, and slightly more prisoners with possible learning or borderline learning disabilities said they didn't know what they would do:

I don't know really. I have been working all my life, I have never been on benefits, but I don't know what I will be allowed to do now.
Scotland, possible learning disabilities

I really don't know what to do. If you don't have parents it's very difficult I want to learn how to talk to people

nicely and learn how to get on with people. If you're not educated there's nothing; working without education is rubbish. I'm not saying I won't work, I'm saying that education is important.
Possible learning disabilities

• Going back to crime

One young offender said:

The things that I wanted to do I can't now because I wanted to go into the army. I expect I'll go back to crime, stuck in a dead end job all my life.

Help making plans

Prisoners were asked if there was somebody who might help them make plans for when they leave prison and over half said there was. Prisoners with possible learning or borderline learning disabilities were the least likely to say there was somebody to help and the comparison group were the most likely.

Of those who said there was somebody who might help, the people and organizations who prisoners referred to included probation/criminal justice social work, housing workers, social/support workers, family and special friends, Job Centre Plus, NACRO/SACRO and personal officers.

Prisoners with learning disabilities or difficulties were more likely to rely on help from statutory services, such as probation/criminal justice social work and social services and the comparison group were more likely to say they would rely on family and friends.

Particular help needed and who might provide it

Prisoners were asked if they knew what sort of help they might need on leaving prison and the majority of prisoners said they did know:

I will need someone to get me a job because I can't do it myself. Last time they sent me to Connexions but on the first day I went they said 'fill this in', and I had to catch a bus by myself and I can't do that. Young offender

> **I can't face leaving and being on the streets again. I am 56 years old and am too vulnerable. I need help but I let them all down.**

I may need help with housing Last time I was released from prison they never gave me anywhere to live.
Possible borderline learning disabilities

We really would both like a care worker, someone to help us. Steve and James live in a place for people with learning difficulties; they get help with their budgeting and all sorts of things.
Possible learning disabilities

I will need to go to a day centre or something, and I will need help with my budgeting and coping with things better.
Scotland

I will need help with washing and cooking.

I need help learning how not to get into trouble, and being able to listen to the judge and probation officers.
Possible learning disabilities

I need help getting used to the outside again. I'll be worried when I leave; I'll probably cross the road and get knocked over. I need to get used to people and places again. You forget it's a big wide world. *Young offender*

When asked who might provide the help, most prisoners were less certain. Of those who responded, an analysis of qualitative data showed that:

- Just under half said they would seek help from 'appropriate'[30] providers of services, which fell to a third for prisoners with possible learning or borderline learning disabilities. The most commonly mentioned source of help was probation/criminal justice social work and expectations were high concerning the level and range of help sought, which included:
  - o finding accommodation
  - o finding work
  - o securing a college place
  - o filling in forms
  - o sorting benefits out
  - o getting used to being out of prison
  - o budgeting

  - o help to stop offending
  - o help with alcohol problems, and
  - o one prisoner said he would ask probation for help making telephone calls.

Based on previous experience, a number of prisoners were not optimistic about help that might be forthcoming from 'appropriate' providers of services:

I don't know who can help really, I saw some worker before but he couldn't help me find a job.
Young offender, possible learning disabilities

Housing should come and see you just before you get out, but all they do is send you to hostel accommodation, it's a vicious circle. *Scotland*

I suppose probation will be able to help but they didn't help before. *Young offender*

- Over a fifth said they didn't know who might help, or that nobody would, or that it was down to them to help themselves.

- Under a fifth said their family or friends would provide any help needed, but it wasn't always clear how realistic this expectation was.

- Under a fifth were vague about who might help and others suggested 'inappropriate'[31] providers of services:

Somebody outside may be able to help.
Scotland

The job club thing can help, but I've not heard back from them, they are supposed to be finding me somewhere to live.
Young offender, possible learning disabilities

And in response to the question, 'who might help?' one prisoner with possible learning disabilities, who said he would need help arranging education on release, said:

There is a woman who works at an African food shop; she might be able to help.

---

[30] 'Appropriate': organizations suggested by the prisoner likely to provide the type of help sought.
[31]. 'Inappropriate': organizations suggested by the prisoner unlikely to provide the type of help sought.

Worries about leaving prison

Prisoners were asked if there was anything that worried them about leaving prison. Over half said they had worries about leaving prison, which rose to two thirds for those with possible learning disabilities. Less than half of the comparison group said they had worries about leaving prison.

Prisoners worried about a range of things, including not being able to cope on release; finding work; the possibility of coming back into prison; not having anywhere to live on release or being sent to live at a hostel; going back to their 'old ways', for example mixing with the wrong crowd or going back to drug or alcohol abuse; being identified in their new community as a former prisoner, and having to start again, often on their own and from scratch:

`I worry about missing appointments (with his probation officer`[32]`), it would be better if they came to visit me. I don't want to get into trouble for missing an appointment.` Possible learning disabilities

`I'm only worrying about the hostel that I might have to live in.` Possible learning disabilities

`It's going to be hard. In here there are no responsibilities. Outside I have got to think about bills, food, getting a job. They don't prepare you for that. I have only got social services for another year and then I have to be sorted.`
Young offender

`Being homeless basically; it's scary when you are homeless. You don't know where you are going to be from day to day.`

Did prisoners think they might come back to prison?

Prisoners were asked if they thought they might come back to prison and if so, what might help them to stay out of trouble. More than one in ten prisoners said they thought they might come back to prison which rose to almost one in three for prisoners with possible learning disabilities, which included the prisoner worried about missing appointments with probation:

`Well, maybe because if I miss an appointment (with probation) I will have to come back. I don't think I will because I am going to try my best to keep to the appointments.` Possible learning disabilities

What might help prisoners to stay out of trouble?

The aspirations of prisoners as they prepared to leave prison, help sought on leaving prison, worries about leaving prison and what would help them to stay out of trouble were similar, namely:

- *something constructive to do during the day, preferably paid work*
- *contact with family and friends*
- *appropriate support on release, in particular help with drug and alcohol abuse and help with daily living*
- *somewhere to live, a home.*

Something constructive to do during the day
Over a quarter said something constructive to do during the day would help them to stay out of trouble, in particular a job, although many were skeptical about their chances of finding paid work:

`Having a job will help me to stay out of trouble, but I can't get a job because I have a criminal record.` Young offender

Contact with family members and friends
Around a fifth said that support from or being able to support family members or friends would help:

`A nice job and a baby will help me to stay out of trouble; it would give me something to look after.`
Young offender, possible learning disabilities

`If I go and stay with my big cousin I will stay out of trouble. We are in a band together, my cousin sings and I play the drums.`
Scotland, young offender, possible learning disabilities

`My girlfriend will help me to stay out of trouble, having some love and support. I have been in care homes all my life. I`

---

32. The prisoner is in prison for breaching his community order for missing appointments with his probation officer. He is unable to read or write.

met my girl, fell in love and I changed, I was doing well. Young offender

Appropriate support on release, in particular help with drug and alcohol abuse and help with daily living
Just under a fifth of prisoners said they would need this sort of help:

I have to keep away from girls and drugs and keep away from the pub. I will keep away from stupid things.
Possible learning disabilities

I may need a mentor; I will probably ask one of the governors on my landing, I'll ask their advice. The Princes Trust said they could help with mentors.

I'm going to see my CPN (community psychiatric nurse) and I'm going to get anger management classes. I think that will help. Woman prisoner, possible learning disabilities

Somewhere to live, a home
Smaller numbers, one in ten, said having somewhere to call 'home' would help:

If I get housing, that will keep me out of trouble but due to my fire raising charge housing workers won't touch me.
Scotland, possible learning disabilities

Having somewhere to live might keep me out of trouble as if you're homeless you're nowhere and where I was sleeping the people around me were all on drugs and stuff. Woman offender

Prisoners also said that staying away from certain people and geographical areas would help to keep them out of trouble; others felt it was down to them to make their own arrangements rather than relying on others and some said that the skills and knowledge they had learned while in prison would help:

Just myself, I don't want to come back. All the courses I have done in here will help me 100%. I don't want to create any more victims; I am a totally different person now.

Having a job will help me to stay out of trouble...but I can't get a job because I have a criminal record.
Young offender

Prisoners' suggestions for what might help

At certain points during the interview prisoners were asked what might have helped them in that particular situation. On occasion prisoners made suggestions about what could be changed. Although prisoners were not asked about what might have helped at the police station, one offender suggested that police suspects should be asked, as a matter of routine, whether they can read and write and, by implication, whether they might need any help.

What might have helped in court?

Prisoners were asked what might have helped in court. One young prisoner with possible learning disabilities said:

I don't know, I give up. I don't care what they do to me any more.

An analysis of qualitative data showed that

- Over a third said the use of simpler language in court and having things explained to them would have helped, which more than doubled for prisoners with possible learning or borderline learning disabilities. None of the comparison group said this:

If someone had explained in my language what things meant this would have helped, for example, lewd, libidinous, bail. I asked my mum but she didn't understand either. Scotland, woman prisoner

There should have been people there telling me what was going to happen. One of the security officers told me what to say and do. He told me to stand up and say my name.

I would have liked someone to have sat down with me for ten minutes to explain to me rather than waffling on and not knowing what they are talking about. Someone who doesn't talk in riddles and understands you.

One prisoner noted that despite having lots of people around to provide support, he was left none the wiser:

I had a lot of people come to visit, the solicitor, social services and loads of visitors that weren't telling me anything.

- A fifth would have liked more support, both practical, including time to think, and moral. None of the comparison group said this:

It's hard making points when you can't write a list. I couldn't read my statement and I wanted to read it again to check what I said was right.

They should let people with special needs sit close to their counsel so they can tell them what they want to say.

I didn't go into the witness box; the judge thought I was being difficult. I should have had someone to help me with my stutter. Young offender

I was nervous, maybe if I had someone to talk to it would have been good. Young offender, possible learning disabilities

- Four prisoners said that better legal advice or a different solicitor would have helped.

- One prisoner thought that awareness training for the judiciary and other court staff might have helped:

A better all round awareness of how dyslexics process information. I brought this up in my appeal and it was dismissed.

What might have helped in prison?

Prisoners were asked about the kinds of support needs they had and what might help them while in prison. An analysis of qualitative data showed that around half of prisoners had positive ideas about what would help; prisoners with possible learning or borderline learning disabilities were the most likely to have positive ideas about what would help.

A number of practical suggestions were made to help overcome difficulties reading prison information and filling in forms, for example increasing the font size, printing onto plain white paper, creating more space on prison forms, making forms 'less scary' and using simpler language:

I do this OK (filling in visiting forms) but the boxes are small and it's hard to squeeze the writing in. I used to get lots retained because they couldn't read them. If all three people have the same address you can spread it out more. Woman prisoner

I get somebody to help me fill in the visiting forms as it's black writing on red paper and that's really hard for me to see. Woman prisoner

A number of prisoners said that more accessible prison forms and information would reduce their need for support.

Prisoners also cited a number of personal support needs and two main themes emerged, which were:

1. help with personal problems and difficulties, including one to one support and asking prisoners for their views
2. less time when there was nothing to do and more constructive things to do.

What prisoners said was not always directly linked to personal support needs, many also made suggestions for how things could be improved more generally. Where positive ideas were made, these have been included.

1. Help with personal problems and difficulties

Almost a half said what would help would be somebody who they could talk to about personal problems and difficulties. Sometimes prisoners wanted specialist help and support, for example with dyslexia and coping with personal trauma and on other occasions the opportunity to talk more generally to somebody and be listened to; some prisoners talked specifically about one to one help, often adding, so that other prisoners wouldn't get to know about their difficulties. Some prisoners were clear about support needing to come from somebody unconnected with the prison and on other occasions prisoners suggested that the person who could help might be a prison officer.
The types of support looked for by prisoners included help with sentence progression, filling in forms, making plans for the future, reading and writing,

staying in touch with family members and the opportunity and the time to talk to somebody they could trust, safe in the knowledge that what they said would go no further. There were no prisoners in the comparison group who said they needed help with personal problems and difficulties, although one did comment on why she thought such help for people with learning disabilities or difficulties was important:

For people with learning difficulties they have Toe-by-Toe. There is also a class for people with learning disabilities but the girls are fed up with it, all they do is colour books and that's not good enough. There's still a lot of stigma attached to Toe-by-Toe and a lot of girls don't want it known that they do it. There should be a way to take people off the wing so that everyone can't see that they can't read. They get called names and picked on.
Woman prisoner, comparison group.

Some examples of what might help

There should be officers on the wings who don't open doors who can help you. There are two on the wings who are really good and they do help you. Like when I split from my girlfriend, I had a talk with one of them. Young offender

We should have someone who has time to come over and find out what's happening and talk to us rather than just being put in a suicide cell someone to take the time and be more understanding.
Scotland, possible learning disabilities

I would like someone to have a sit down and talk with, to tell me what's happening and how to do things.
Young offender

I would like to get a job, learn how to read and write. That's what I have been trying to do.
Young offender, possible learning disabilities

It would help if someone would help me make a phone call and help me sort my sentence plan. I am also having nightmares and waking up frightened in the night. Woman prisoner

One prisoner said that while certain support was available it didn't necessarily come at the right time:

> **I would have liked reading and writing classes and I would have also liked to have worked. I'm in my cell for 23 hours a day.**
> Young offender, possible learning disabilities

There is a lot of support coming in, like throughcare but if people need help for housing there's no use if they come to see you at the last minute and you end up in a hostel. Scotland

One to one support

A number of prisoners talked specifically about the need for one-to-one support, which in the main was to prevent other prisoners being made aware of their support needs and the consequent risk of victimization.

People should help you with stuff, like reading and writing, you should get one on one help. You feel out of place if you can't read and write because people laugh at you. Young offender, possible learning disabilities

You should have someone who comes to the wing to help you and then you would just have help from one person that would be much better. If people see you getting help they might laugh at you and then pick on you. There should be somewhere quiet where nobody can see you. You would find that people use it a lot more. Even one of the screws could do it for like an hour or something.
Young offender, possible learning disabilities

I would like to do a one on one to help me read and write. In my class I am the lowest person there and they are teaching things that are above me. I don't know where I am going to or coming from sometimes. Possible learning disabilities

It would be good to be able to sit down and talk to someone and get help to fill in forms, like someone unrelated to the prison, not staff or other inmates it would help to be given definite dates and appointments for this. Scotland

Asking prisoners for their views

A number suggested that prison staff should ask prisoners about their personal support needs and for their views on what might help:

I don't think they ask people if they can read or write when they come in, they should as lots of people can't. I can and I'm one of the lucky ones.

They've everything here but they don't ask you, it does your head in. (the interviewer asked, 'what do you mean, "don't ask you"?') They don't ask for our views.
Young offender

2. Less time with nothing to do and more constructive things to do

One in five said that less time when there was nothing to do and more constructive things to do would help. Prisoners with possible learning or borderline learning disabilities were the most likely to say this. Time alone, with nothing to do made prisoners feel depressed, frustrated and angry. Several prisoners, in particular young prisoners, said more help learning to read and write would help:

I just wish I could learn to read and write, that would be fun, wicked. It's what holds me back really.
Young offender, possible learning disabilities

I need help with reading I don't know if education offers it. Young offender

There should be more things for you to do in the units, like activities but there's nothing for you to do. There's in-cell hobbies but we have to fill in a form for this too.
Scotland, woman prisoner, possible learning disabilities

There needs to be something more done to help prisoners progress themselves, so that criminals don't go back to criminal activity Getting education isn't enough; you need something for self-employment. You never get a job with a criminal record. We're all human and can make mistakes. We're not evil.

Conclusion

Main Findings

This research set out to hear from prisoners with learning disabilities and learning difficulties about their experiences of the criminal justice system. Prisoners were also asked about their life immediately prior to being arrested and aspirations for the future. Interviews with prisoners without such impairments have enabled comparisons to be drawn.

Main findings:

1. **Reading**: over two-thirds of prisoners had difficulties reading prison information, which rose to four-fifths for prisoners with possible learning disabilities[33]; similar difficulties were likely to have occurred at the police station and in court.

2. **Writing**: over two-thirds of prisoners had difficulties filling in prison forms, which rose to over three-quarters for those with possible learning disabilities ; similar difficulties were likely to have occurred at the police station and in court.

3. **Understanding and being understood:**

   a. results from the LIPS screening tool show that over two-thirds of prisoners experienced difficulties in verbal comprehension skills, including difficulties understanding certain words and in expressing themselves

   b. over half of prisoners said they had difficulties making themselves understood in prison, which rose to more then two-thirds for those with possible learning disabilities; similar difficulties were likely to have occurred at the police station and in court.

Before being arrested

4. Prisoners were almost twice as likely as the comparison group to have been unemployed prior to arrest.

5. Education: prisoners were

   a. three times as likely to have been excluded from school as the comparison group, and

   b. over half said they had attended a special school.

At the police station

6. Less than a third of prisoners received support from an appropriate adult (AA) during police interview and none appeared to have benefited from special measures such as the support of an intermediary.

7. Prisoners were more likely to say they received help from a solicitor rather than an AA while at the police station and a third said they had been helped a lot.

8. Half of prisoners with possible learning disabilities said they didn't know what would happen to them once they had been charged.

9. Some prisoners said:

   a. they had been beaten or handled roughly by the police[34]

   b. they felt suicidal or thought about self harm

   c. they felt manipulated into agreeing to a police interview without support[35]

   d. they were denied their medication[36].

At Court

10. Over a fifth of prisoners said they didn't understand what was going on in court or what was happening to them; some prisoners didn't understand why they were in court or what they had done wrong.

11. A fifth of prisoners said more support in court would have helped including practical and moral support.

12. Over a third of prisoners said the use of simpler language in court and having things explained to them would have helped.

---

33. Prisoners with possible learning and borderline learning disabilities are described as having 'possible learning disabilities' in this section

34. This finding corresponds with evidence submitted by PRT to the Joint Committee on Human Rights, June 2007

35. ibid

36. ibid

In prison

13. Despite there being no routine or systematic screening tool or assessment to identify prisoners with learning disabilities, almost half of those identified by the LIPS screening tool were also identified by prison staff, but this identification rarely led to support measures.

14. Over half of prisoners said they had been scared while in prison.

15. Almost half of prisoners said they had been bullied and that people had been nasty to them; none of the comparison group said this.

16. Over half of prisoners were attending education classes and those with possible learning disabilities were the most likely to be attending classes.

17. Prisoners with possible low average IQ were the least likely to have a job in prison.

18. Prisoners with possible learning disabilities were the least likely to:

    a. know when their parole or release date was

    b. be in touch with family and friends

    c. ask someone if they didn't understand what was happening

    d. know what they would do if they felt unwell

    e. know how to make a complaint

    f. have participated in cognitive behaviour treatment programmes.

19. Prisoners with possible learning disabilities were the most likely to:

    a. spend time alone and have fewer things to do

    b. have positive ideas about the kinds of support that would help them while in prison.

20. Prisoners with learning disabilities or difficulties were five times as likely as those in the comparison group to have been subject to control and restraint techniques.

21. Prisoners with learning disabilities or difficulties were more than three times as likely as the comparison group to have spent time in segregation.

22. Depression and anxiety

    a. prisoners with learning disabilities or difficulties were almost three times as likely as the comparison group to have clinically significant depression

    b. prisoners with learning disabilities or difficulties were almost three times as likely as the comparison group to have clinically significant anxiety.

The future

23. Prisoners expressed a wide and varied range of aspirations for the future including finding work, going to college, spending time with family and friends, 'sorting themselves out', 'doing better', finding somewhere to live and generally getting on with life.

24. Prisoners with possible learning disabilities were the most likely to say they had worries about leaving prison and that they thought they might come back.

25. Prisoners with possible learning disabilities were the least likely to say there was somebody to help them make plans for when they left prison.

26. Prisoners were generally uncertain about where they would go for particular help as they prepared to leave prison, especially those with possible learning disabilities , and had high expectations of the kinds and extent of help they might expect from probation/criminal justice social work, to the point that many had expectations that were unrealistic.

Concluding Discussion

Overarching themes

During the three year *No One Knows* programme five overarching themes have emerged, which are:

*   disability discrimination and possible human rights abuses

*   knowing who has learning disabilities or difficulties

*   implications for the criminal justice system

*   a needs led approach: collaborative multi-agency working

*   workforce development.

These will be discussed first followed by two further issues:

*   diversion from the criminal justice system of people with learning disabilities

*   children with learning disabilities or difficulties and statutory education.

The likely 'double discrimination' of black and minority ethnic people with learning disabilities or difficulties who get into trouble with the police has not been covered by *No One Knows* and the requirement for further research is noted on page 74.

The following discussion relates to the four UK nations. Although there are some references to nation specific policy, these have been kept to a minimum.

1. Disability discrimination and possible human rights abuses

Evidence from this study, *Prisoners' Voices*, earlier research from *No One Knows* and the report, *A Life Like Any Other?* published by the Joint Committee on Human Rights, demonstrate that people with learning disabilities or difficulties are discriminated against personally, systemically and routinely as they enter and travel through the criminal justice system (Talbot, 2007; Loucks, 2007; Joint Committee on Human Rights, June 2007).

Whether through ignorance, a willingness to be complicit or both, criminal justice staff and those responsible for criminal justice services are failing in their duty to promote equality of opportunity and to eliminate discrimination and, as such, are not complying with the requirements of the Disability Discrimination Act (2005) and the disability equality duty in particular (DED).

A recent report into disabled people's experiences of hate crime in the UK found that 'casual and institutional disablism is rife in our society'. The report goes on to say that this 'creates an environment where disability hate crime can occur without being recognized or challenged. It also means mainstream services often fail to meet disabled people's access and information needs.' (Quarmby, 2008).

This resonates with much of the evidence reported by *No One Knows*. Far too many instances of disability discrimination and possible human rights abuses have emerged. Four instances of greatest concern are listed below; all require further investigation[37]:

*   maltreatment of people with learning disabilities and learning difficulties by the police[38] and by prison officers

*   the lack of an appropriate adult[39] for vulnerable suspects during police interview

---

37. See also, PRT briefing paper, Human rights and offenders with learning difficulties and learning disabilities (Watson, 2007)
38. See also Joint Committee on Human Rights, A life like any other? Paragraph 210
39. For England and Wales, the Police and Criminal Evidence Act (PACE) Code C requires that an AA is called to the police station if a person who is 'mentally disordered or otherwise mentally vulnerable' has been detained. AAs are also required for detainees under 17 years of age.

- defendants with learning disabilities and learning difficulties being unaware of what is happening to them during their trial and an inability to understand decisions of the court[40]
- prison information and regimes that are inaccessible to prisoners with learning disabilities and difficulties.[41]

The DED has the dual aim of eliminating discrimination and promoting equality, thus criminal justice agencies must work to ensure that discrimination does not occur by making adjustments to existing provision and ensuring that future provision is accessible to people with disabilities, including those with learning disabilities and difficulties. In other words, the likelihood of discrimination should be anticipated and action taken to prevent it from happening.

Earlier research by *No One Knows*, and this study in particular, provide some very clear indications where 'reasonable adjustments' could be made to prevent disability discrimination. Two of the most obvious examples perhaps being making all criminal justice information, including forms, posters and letters available in 'easy read' and advocacy support.

Given the often extreme difficulties that prisoners experienced in accessing and understanding information and in being able to make themselves understood, routine access to advocacy support throughout the criminal justice system would ensure a much greater inclusion of people with learning disabilities and difficulties than has hitherto been realized. This could be provided, for example, by extending and further developing AA provision that is available to vulnerable detainees at the police station. The availability of such support could also highlight, on an ongoing basis, where further adjustments need to be made.

Promoting disability equality and preventing discrimination is not about treating a few people differently once discrimination has occurred, or bolting on bits of extra support that at best provide the chance of a second class service. It is about changing the way things are done: the DDA requires systems and procedures to change to ensure that individuals with disabilities feel the effects of their disability less or not at all.

2. Knowing who has learning disabilities or difficulties

The first step in ensuring that people with learning disabilities or difficulties are appropriately dealt with when they get into trouble with the police is being able to identify who they are. There are various points at which this could happen as people enter and travel through the criminal justice system. However there is no effective, routine or systematic procedure for doing so (Talbot 2007; Loucks, 2007; Jacobson, 2008).

Learning disabilities and difficulties are largely 'hidden disabilities' with few visual or behavioural clues. Many people with such disabilities try hard to hide their impairments and even if asked directly, especially by people they don't know or in a stressful environment, may deny that they have learning disabilities or difficulties.

Notwithstanding problems of identification, public authorities are required by the DDA (2005) to be proactive in eliminating discrimination and promoting equality; thus changes in how criminal justice agencies conduct themselves and carry out their work should be made to ensure that provision is accessible to people with disabilities.

The first point of contact that suspects have with the criminal justice system is generally at the police station and it is here that people with learning disabilities in particular, and people with learning difficulties should be identified. There are a number of reasons for this, the most fundamental being to ensure justice; the right to a fair trial as protected by common law and enshrined in Article 6 of the European Convention on Human Rights (ECHR).

---

40. See also Joint Committee on Human Rights, A life like any other? Paragraph 212
41. ibid

For some people with learning disabilities (not learning difficulties unless other factors apply, for example mental illness) the possibility of diversion from the criminal justice system may apply, see pages 67 and 72.

There are a number of developments in the possible use of screening tools and questions to identify people with learning disabilities or difficulties.

Most police forces ask detainees prescribed questions to determine whether they are 'vulnerable' and therefore in need of an appropriate adult (AA). In one study (Clare, 2003) a series of questions were developed to help custody sergeants decide when an AA should be called due to a detainee possibly having learning disabilities. These questions have been used by the Metropolitan Police (Form 57M) and will be incorporated into the next upgrade of the National Strategy for Police Information Systems (NSPIS), which forms part of the risk assessment undertaken for detainees in most police forces in England and Wales.

Towards the end of 2008, it is anticipated that a screening tool for learning disabilities will be piloted at three prisons in England under the auspices of the Department of Health. A 'hidden disabilities' questionnaire, developed jointly by Dyslexia Action and the Learning and Skills Council is being piloted, and a current study being undertaken by Research Autism and the University of Edinburgh to determine the prevalence of autistic spectrum disorder in Scottish prisons will also develop a screening tool to be used by prison officers.

Such moves are very positive but developing a screening tool or tools is only part of the solution; consideration must also be given to how the tool(s) will be used. Busy police stations and overcrowded prisons may be persuaded to use one screening tool; staff are unlikely to use three. And yet each screening tool would add significantly to the understanding by criminal justice staff of how best to support prisoners and when referrals to staff with relevant professional expertise, for example in healthcare and education, are appropriate.

For screening tools to work systems and structures must be embedded to ensure they are used properly, routinely and systematically. Clarity is required on which screening tools should be used when and by whom and with what result. Further, it must be recognized that, while screening tools will identify most of the people they are designed to, not everyone will be identified in this way. Criminal justice staff will need to remain alert to the probability that there will be other prisoners in need of support and possible referral to specialist services.

Linked to the identification of people with learning disabilities or difficulties is the issue of information flow – the sharing of appropriate information as the offender travels through the criminal justice system. Earlier research from *No One Knows* found that such information was rarely passed on. For example, even if the police decided it was necessary to secure the services of an AA at the police station, this information is unlikely to 'arrive' with the offender upon his entry into prison; thus, information that might usefully inform an offender's support needs is rarely available (Talbot, 2007; Loucks, 2007).

Effective information sharing and information sharing protocols between the different criminal justice agencies and between criminal justice, offender health, and offender learning are necessary to ensure that people with learning disabilities or difficulties are supported appropriately as they enter and travel though the criminal justice system.

3. Implications for the criminal justice system

Notwithstanding the risk of non-compliance with disability and human rights legislation there are a number of implications that arise when people with learning disabilities or difficulties are not effectively identified or supported.

The problems most prisoners had with verbal comprehension skills in this study highlights the importance of police officers in particular recognizing the signs of a person 'not understanding' despite their being able to respond to questioning. This has implications for suspects with learning disabilities in particular who are likely to struggle with police questioning and cautions (Clare and Gudjonsson, 1991; Murphy and Mason, 2005), with the result that they may incriminate themselves even if they are innocent (Loucks, 2007). Empirical studies suggest that, compared to their non-disabled peers, people with learning disabilities who get into trouble with the police are less likely to understand information about the caution and legal rights, are more likely to make decisions which would not protect their rights, and are more likely to be acquiescent and suggestible (Clare, 2003).

Despite the difficulties that prisoners had with verbal comprehension skills, fewer than one in three received support from an AA, which is consistent with the generally low levels of take up of AA provision for vulnerable detainees, and none appeared to have benefited from an intermediary to support communication and to facilitate accurate exchange of information.

Two main factors conspire against an AA being called: suspects with support needs going unidentified and a lack of individuals who can perform the role of AA effectively (Jacobson, 2008)[42].

Once in court, despite a general recognition in law that defendants must be able to understand and effectively participate in the criminal proceedings of which they are a part (Jacobson with Seden, forthcoming), one in five prisoners in this study experienced problems understanding what was going on and what was happening to them. For one prisoner, his lack of understanding was so great that he didn't know why he was in court, while another said that although she was aware she had done wrong didn't know quite what.

The Youth Justice and Criminal Evidence Act 1999 contains special measures aimed at safeguarding and protecting vulnerable people in court, for example the provision of intermediaries to facilitate communication. However these are not extended to vulnerable defendants; they are available to vulnerable victims and witnesses only. In effect defendants with support needs are being discriminated against purely on the basis of their status as the accused.

Although a Practice Direction, issued in 2007 by the Lord Chief Justice, outlines a range of measures 'to assist a vulnerable defendant to understand and participate in... proceedings', it doesn't carry the same weight as legislation. Support for vulnerable defendants should be made available on the same statutory footing as that for victims and witnesses and should include advocacy and the use of intermediaries.

In 2007 *No One Knows* submitted evidence to an enquiry being undertaken by the Joint Committee on Human Rights on the human rights of adults with learning disabilities. The evidence submitted included defendants being unaware of what was happening during their trial and an inability to understand decisions of the court. In their subsequent report, *A Life Like Any Other? Human Rights of Adults with Learning Disabilities* the Committee said:

> *We are concerned that the problems highlighted by this evidence could have potentially very serious implications for the rights of people with learning disabilities to a fair hearing, as protected by the common law and by Article 6 ECHR. Some of this evidence also suggests that there are serious failings in the criminal justice system, which gives rise to the discriminatory treatment of people with learning disabilities.* (Paragraph 212, March 2008)

On arrival into prison people with learning disabilities and difficulties face a number of problems due to their impairments. Poor literacy skills and difficulties expressing themselves make daily living and accessing the prison regime problematic. Difficulties in understanding information and being able to complete prison forms in particular leaves them especially vulnerable, pitching them, as it does, on the mercy of other prisoners and prison staff; as one prisoner said, *'everything is one big problem'*.

Further difficulties are caused by the stigma frequently attached to learning disabilities and difficulties and as a result many prisoners try hard to hide their impairments for fear of ridicule, because they feel embarrassed and,

---

42. For England and Wales, the current PACE review (August, 2008) contains proposals to 'professionalize' AA provision and give police authorities the statutory role to ensure that an effective service is operating in their area.

for some, because it is a sign of 'weakness'; 'showing 'weakness' in prison can be a pre-cursor to exploitation and victimization by other prisoners.

The reasons that prisoners in this study were more likely to be bullied than those without such impairments is unclear, although 'showing weakness', difficulties with verbal comprehension skills, and problems with attention deficits and impulsivity associated with ADHD cannot be ruled out. In her review of bullying literature, Ireland (2002) found that estimates of having been a victim of bullying in prison ranged from 30-75 per cent for young offenders and from 8-57 per cent for adults. This broad range suggests that estimates of the prevalence of bullying are inherently vague. Why prisoners with possible learning disabilities may be less vulnerable to bullying are even less clear and this is an area in which further investigation would be valuable.

Because deficits associated with learning disabilities and difficulties are not routinely recognized, resulting problems such as failure to cope with an aspect of the prison regime can be labelled as 'bad' or 'manipulative' behaviour, leading to further negative consequences for the individual prisoner. Prison behaviour deemed disruptive, such as misusing in-cell emergency bells, kicking cell doors, damage to prison property and shouting have been linked to prisoners with learning disabilities (Loucks, 2007; Bryan et al 2004).

The high level of control and restraint techniques used against this group of prisoners reflects the association between poor communication skills and behavioural difficulties (Humber and Snow, 2001) and the attention deficits and impulsivity associated with ADHD. For poor communication skills interventions by speech and language therapists at an early stage have been shown to have far reaching benefits for individual prisoners and for the prison staff working with them (see for example Bryan et al, 2004).

An inability or unwillingness on the part of prisoners to use prison complaints procedures and their propensity to 'take matters into their own hands', which generally meant meeting aggression with aggression, is also likely to result in the increased use of control and restraint techniques and segregation.

That prisoners with a possible low average IQ were the most likely to have been subject to control and restraint techniques and segregation demonstrates the importance of prison services, in particular, responding to individual prisoner need rather than the use of 'labels' or a clinical diagnosis, for example of learning disability, to determine levels of support.

Prisoners' inability to participate fully in the prison regime leaves them at greater psychological risk as they spend more time alone with little to occupy themselves; many experienced high levels of depression and anxiety. Liebling (1992) identified prisoners who spent most of their time in their cells 'doing nothing' as being at most risk of suicide while in custody.

Prisoners' exclusion from cognitive behaviour treatment programmes (Talbot, 2007; Loucks, 2007) makes it less likely that their offending will be addressed and more likely that they will return to prison; their inability to complete such programmes is likely to affect parole and release dates with some prisoners staying in prison longer as a result.

A recent thematic review by HM Chief Inspectors of Prisons and Probation, *The indeterminate sentence for public protection*, described this predicament - prisoners being unable to access the interventions they needed to secure release, as 'Kafka-esque' and recommended that 'interventions to reduce risk are adapted to be suitable for those with learning disability or difficulty.' (HM Chief Inspectors of Prisons and Probation, 2008)

On the same issue, the Joint Committee on Human Rights said:

The evidence which we have received[43] on the treatment of people with learning disabilities in prison and their inability to secure equal access to parole, raises one of the most serious issues in our inquiry. We are deeply concerned that this evidence indicates that, because of a failure to provide for their needs, people with learning

43. From *No One Knows*, Mencap and the Foundation for People with Learning Disabilities

disabilities may serve longer custodial sentences than others convicted of comparable crimes. This clearly engages Article 5 ECHR (right to liberty) and Article 14 (enjoyment of ECHR rights without discrimination). It is also an area that falls within the Prison Service's responsibility under the Disability Equality Duty.
(Paragraph 215, March 2008)

A common thread running through *Prisoners' Voices* was the problem associated with prisoners not being able to access or understand information and consequently not understanding what was happening around them or was expected of them. Whether at the police station, in court or in prison, prisoners frequently didn't quite 'get it' and as a result were left behind – both literally and metaphorically, because nobody cared to listen.

4. A needs led approach: collabortive multi-agency working

Criminal justice agencies alone do not have the requisite expertise to identify adequately, work with and support people with learning disabilities and difficulties. Collaboration is required involving the collective efforts of criminal justice agencies, healthcare, social care, education and the full range of local services.

There is an inherent problem with much service provision that is not just the domain of criminal justice: the 'client' is required to move between different service providers that rarely talk to each other, receiving support according to availability rather than in response to individual need. To ensure the most effective outcome for people with learning disabilities or difficulties who offend, this needs turning on its head. Instead, person centred packages of intervention and support are required, which should be provided in a structured and timely way as the individual enters and travels through the criminal justice system.

This has particular relevance for suspects with learning disabilities when they first come into contact with the police. Home Office circular 66/90 makes it clear that alternatives to prosecution should be considered where the prosecution of an individual with a 'mental disorder' is not in the public interest (Jacobson, 2008). Such alternatives however can only be realized if criminal justice and healthcare work together at the point that an individual comes into contact with the police, and where local provision exists.

Notwithstanding some good examples[44] of collaborative working, there is a paucity of local multi-agency schemes necessary to be able to plan for and execute effective alternatives to prosecution or, if diversion is considered inappropriate, to support people through the criminal justice process.

The Reed Review (1992) called for a 'nationwide provision of properly resourced court assessment and diversion schemes'. These schemes, generally referred to as court diversion and liaison schemes or criminal justice liaison and diversion schemes, would facilitate access to treatment and support for 'mentally disordered' offenders, undertake assessments and provide information to the courts about the support needs of defendants (Jacobson with Seden, forthcoming).

However only around a third of magistrates' courts in England and Wales have access to such provision and those schemes that do exist rarely have learning disability expertise or ready access to it (NACRO, 2005).

Where good practice does exist it is often dependent on individual staff rather than on formal systems or structural framework.

Once sentenced, either to a custodial or a community sentence, the opportunity arises to address the needs of offenders through person centred packages of intervention and support. To an extent, the framework for this already exists – offender management and sentence planning, but some refining is necessary.

For example, criminal justice staff are not always aware of what support is available or could be provided. Research from *No One Knows* found that even within individual prisons, staff were often unaware of support available for prisoners with learning disabilities or difficulties outside of that provided by their own department. Staff knew about prisoners only in the context of their own department or area of responsibility, for example as offender-learners or in residential areas - on the wings or landings; the prisoner was rarely 'centre stage'. The few exceptions to this, where there were some good examples of multi-agency, multi-disciplinary working, were mostly found in the women's and young offender estates (Talbot, 2007).

Two early recommendations made by *No One Knows* were for multi-disciplinary approaches to meeting the support needs of prisoners and for each prison to develop a matrix of available support, including access to services in the wider community (Talbot, 2007; Loucks, 2007; Loucks, 2008).

Once in prison, however, the reality is that prisoners are generally out of sight and out of mind of local services. Notwithstanding the need for greater collaboration between prisons and local services, there is also the need for clarity on what prisons can reasonably expect of local services both to support prisoners while they are in prison and crucially, as they prepare for, and upon, release.

The support needs of many prisoners in this study were met by fellow inmates; similar findings were recently reported in the Health Service Journal (Tabreham, 2008), which found that prisoners routinely cared for others who were elderly, vulnerable or ill and that there was a lack of support for those who took on such a caring role.

There are a number of factors that should be considered in regard to prisoners acting as carers or supporters. For example, it would be inappropriate for prisons to rely on the unrecognized and unsupported efforts of prisoners to meet their responsibilities under the DDA, in particular the DED. While it is likely that the majority of prisoners providing support to those in need will do so in the spirit of 'good citizenship', the possibility that some might have ulterior motives should not be ignored. Indeed, one prisoner in this study was told she should not rely on other prisoners for support.

There are schemes whereby prisoners volunteer to help other inmates, two such examples being Toe-by-Toe and Samaritan Listeners. These schemes, which are lead by voluntary sector organizations, work with prison staff to plan the volunteering and provide training and support for the prisoner-volunteers. A similar scheme could be devised to recruit prisoner-volunteers as supporters and carers for prisoners in need of support, for example with routine 'daily living', which might involve help filling in forms, explaining how things are done in prison and advocacy. As with all such schemes, and notwithstanding the valued efforts of prisoners, their volunteering should supplement, rather than replace or be instead of, necessary services and provision that are the responsibility of the prison or of health and social care to provide.

In considering the needs of prisoners with learning disabilities the use of separate units within the prison has been suggested. There are potential risks as well as benefits associated with this. One risk is the chance of an impoverished regime for prisoners not living in the mainstream. Another lies in the possibility of a separate unit being co-located with prisoners kept apart from the main prison for reasons of personal safety, for example prisoners who are sex offenders, which may place a prisoner with learning disabilities in an even more vulnerable situation than remaining on main location.

One member of the Working for Justice Group spoke graphically of his horror at being placed in a vulnerable prisoner unit and the grave risks, as he saw it, in being associated, in the minds of other prisoners, with sex offenders. He asked to be returned to the main prison.

One prison in England is developing a therapeutic community approach to working with prisoners with learning disabilities and it will be interesting to know the results.

In the meantime, if it is not possible to provide adequate support, so enabling prisoners to live alongside others on the wings or landings, there is a strong argument that they should be diverted away from criminal justice into a more appropriate setting.

Effective resettlement plans are important for prisoners with learning disabilities in particular, and for those with learning difficulties as they prepare for release. But how well prisoners are prepared is not encouraging. A Home Office study (2005) found that one in five prisoners who needed help with accommodation actually received support or advice; two-thirds of prisoners without accommodation arranged on release had not received any advice, and only half of those who had received some form of help had an address to go to on release. The study concluded that 'many prisoners would like help looking for accommodation but do not receive it' (Bromley Briefings, page 36, reference 364, June 2008).

People with learning disabilities are most likely to 'qualify' for support services on release from prison and the importance of alerting the local authority area from which the prisoner came or to which he will return cannot be overemphasized. Appropriate social care and support takes a long time to set up and arrangements for release need to start from the beginning of a prisoner's sentence[45].

Preventing people from getting into trouble in the first place is the ideal but access to support services that might help is not straightforward. Reduced local budgets and increases in the cost of service provision often mean that as the 'cake' gets smaller services are able to work with fewer people and consequently target those with the most severe or complex support needs. Local services frequently have differing criteria for access to support, which means that a person with learning disabilities in one area might receive support, while in another he would not. Often the support needs of such people are of a relatively low level, for example help with budgeting, paying bills, personal care and friendship networks[46], but they are long term. Quite low levels of support can make all the difference between a person staying on the right side of the law and getting involved in risky and offending behaviour.

Local services are not always willing or able to work with people with challenging behaviour – especially if they are not known to services, and in many areas there is no learning disability forensic service or forensic expertise; local drug and alcohol services may not offer programmes designed or adapted for people with low cognitive ability or poor literacy or communication skills, and multi-agency working between criminal justice, healthcare and other local services to prevent offending is rare.

For many people local support services simply don't exist. For example, in the absence of other factors such as mental illness, it is unlikely that a person with learning difficulties, including high functioning Asperger syndrome and ADHD, or low average IQ would be able to access statutory support, even if the support required might be very low level or short term to prevent or ameliorate a crisis.

A small but significant number of prisoners in this study 'got caught' in order to access services in prison they were unable to access in the community, in particular help with drug and alcohol abuse. One young offender with possible learning disabilities saw being in prison as an opportunity to provide his family with some respite and another said he preferred prison, describing it as a 'a big family'. The fact that most who spoke in such terms were young prisoners engenders a particularly acute sense of despair both in the community services that had so clearly failed to deliver and in the lack of essential service provision.

Eligibility criteria for support should be flexible and inclusive; they should not be used to exclude people and to ration services. National standards for health and social care provision are necessary, including clear guidance and accountability for transition arrangements between children's and adult services. People who offend should not be denied access to services on the basis of their offending behaviour or because they have previously been an offender.

In earlier research from *No One Knows*, one head of learning and skills described the phrase, 'from existing resources' as being 'threadbare' (Talbot, 2007). A needs led approach to preventing offending and preventing re-offending could, in part, come from a re-ordering of existing resources, but a greater level of investment is required. Perhaps of even greater importance, however, is an inter-ministerial commitment to collaborative

45. See also Prison Service Journal, *Getting health and community care to prisoners who will need it on release*; *Positive Practice Positive Outcomes* and PSA Delivery Agreement 16: increase the proportion of socially excluded adults in settled accommodation and employment, education or training.
46. KeyRing Living Support Networks is a good example, there are others

working and a mandatory requirement for effective multi-agency working at the local level. The ministerial departments should include health and social care, local government, children and families and the justice agencies.

5. Workforce development

Following publication of the *No One Knows* report on the views of prison staff in Scotland (Loucks, 2007) the Scottish Prison Service formed a partnership with Capability Scotland to develop guidance for supporting prisoners with disabilities. They have also established a multi-agency, multi-disciplinary working group to consider the needs of prisoners with learning disabilities and difficulties while they are in prison and upon release.

For the Northern Ireland Prison Service, early work has focused on effective interventions for prisoners with dyslexia, including training for staff.

The most consistent message from the Working for Justice Group has been the need for awareness training on learning disabilities and difficulties for criminal justice staff, followed by a concern that many people working in public services, including in education and healthcare, don't really understand what a learning disability is or what support a person with learning disabilities might need. Prison staff themselves recognize the need for such training, including during initial training for prison officers and specialist training for staff in specific roles (Talbot 2007; Loucks 2007).

As a result of the first *No One Knows* report (Talbot, 2007), a one day awareness training workshop on learning disabilities and difficulties for prison staff was developed under the auspices of the Department of Health, with the initiative being led by the Valuing People Support Team (South East). The workshop, which is co-delivered by people with learning disabilities has been piloted and will be made available to three members of staff at all establishments in England and Wales during 2009. As part of the same initiative, a two hour module was planned for inclusion in the prison officer entry level training (POELT). However, due to the prison service's 'workforce modernization' this may no longer be the case.

The one day workshop has been adapted for staff working with under 18 year olds in prison in England and Wales, is currently being adapted for probation staff, and discussions are taking place to adapt the workshop for court staff.

The extent to which awareness training on learning disabilities and difficulties is available for police personnel varies but opportunities do exist during initial training for all new recruits, as part of race and diversity training and training for custody officers (Jacobson, 2008). There are examples where joint training between police and healthcare yield positive results, one such example is between the Northumbria Police and the Northumberland, Tyne and Wear NHS Trust[47].

The publication in 2007 of *Positive Practice, Positive Outcomes,* by Offender Health, provides useful information for professionals in the criminal justice system working with offenders with learning disabilities[48].

Taking a broader view of awareness training, staff should also undertake training in the statutory equality duties required of public authorities, which would help to ensure they don't inadvertently discriminate, or allow people in their care to discriminate, against others.

Raising awareness is important; it alerts staff to the possibility of people having learning disabilities or difficulties and encourages them to question what might be behind certain behaviours, for example apparent non-compliance that may hide a lack of understanding on the part of the offender. Staff are also likely to become more confident in providing support and in making referrals for more specialist help.

47. See www.prisonreformtrust.org.uk/nok; case studies
48. See, http://www.kc.csip.org.uk/index.php

Prison staff, officers in particular, can make all the difference for prisoners in need of support – two different approaches taken by officers are highlighted below:

```
One officer always helps me, he's a nice man. He talks to me too.

You can ask the screws for help, but they just laugh at you.
```

Some prisoners in this study spoke warmly of officers describing them as their *'gaol dad'* or *'mum number two'*; one young offender said of an officer, *'what a guy!'* Clearly all were officers who provided much needed support. There were however many more examples where officers were either unwilling or unable, possibly because of restraints on time, to provide any help. There were also far too many examples where officers were clearly unkind in their response to requests for help, including 'laughing along' with other members of staff and prisoners. Such behaviour on the part of staff fosters the 'environment where disability hate crime can occur' (Quarmby, 2008) and should be stopped.

The role of prison officers in providing support should be clarified. For example, is providing support to prisoners part of a prison officer's duty, or is it an optional extra only to be undertaken should officers have the time, the confidence or indeed the inclination to provide it? If providing support is integral to officers' duties, appropriate training should be provided, and standards set and monitored.

The use of screening tools for learning disabilities and difficulties and awareness training for prison staff is likely to prompt higher levels of referrals for specialist help, for example from healthcare and education. In response to this, relevant professional expertise needs to be readily available across the criminal justice system. However there are big gaps in service provision. (Talbot, 2007; Loucks, 2007; Loucks, 2008).

As criminal justice agencies know more about the support needs of offenders they will be better able to provide detailed information to inform service provision. The role of commissioners is important here. One example of where commissioners have taken a proactive approach is South Staffordshire PCT. The PCT is responsible for the commissioning of mental health and specialist services, including learning disability, at six prisons. The South Staffordshire prison health partnership board, of which the PCT is a member, has commissioned an independent review of learning disability services across the six prisons to identify, amongst other things:

• how existing services can be developed to better support the needs of prisoners with a learning disability

• how different departments within the prison, for example education, residential, healthcare and resettlement can work together to support the needs of prisoners with a learning disability

• gaps in healthcare services for prisoners with a learning disability, and

• to provide recommendations to inform future commissioning plans.

Preventative strategies should be a fundamental component in commissioning services. If the needs of offenders with learning disabilities or difficulties are viewed from a developmental perspective then it is essential that any underlying cognitive delays and deficits are identified and addressed as early as possible. This requires collaboration between, amongst others, local schools and education services, child and adolescent mental health services (CAMHS) and youth offending services.

Collaborative multi-agency working brings its own challenges. The organizational cultures of agencies involved are very different and the staff who work in them will not necessarily know about, or appreciate, the different areas of expertise, and policy and legislative opportunities and limitations of the other agencies involved.

Joint multi-agency and multi-disciplinary training, such as that undertaken between the Northumbria Police and the Northumberland, Tyne and Wear NHS Trust, not only provides opportunities to learn together and to foster joint working, it also enables professionals and practitioners to begin to 'know what they don't know' about the other parts of the 'system', which together has collective responsibility for, and the route to, local solutions.

Across the board, staff require a much greater awareness and clearer guidance on what courses of action are available or expected of them in deciding how to act in the best interests of people with learning disabilities or difficulties.

For example, in her research Jacobson (2008) found that decision making on enforcement, diversion and disposal options of police suspects with learning disabilities was inconsistent, as was the clinical attention received from healthcare professionals at the police station. Anecdotal evidence from prison healthcare suggests that staff often don't know what factors they should take into account when considering diversion from the criminal justice system for prisoners with learning disabilities or how they would go about doing so, and prison staff appointed to ensure that the needs of prisoners with disabilities are met (disability liaison officers in England and Wales) often receive little guidance or training on how to fulfill their role.

Two further issues for discussion:

• diversion from the criminal justice system of people with learning disabilities
• children with learning disabilities and difficulties and statutory education.

6. Diversion from the criminal justice system of people with learning disabilities

The police have a substantial degree of discretion in deciding what action to take when it appears an offence has been committed by an identifiable individual, including diversion away from the criminal justice system. There is however disagreement amongst police officers, health and social care workers and legal practitioners (and others) about the appropriateness of a suspect with learning disabilities being dealt with by the criminal justice system or being diverted away from it. This, to a degree, reflects a lack of clarity in current policy and guidance on the application of the concept of criminal responsibility to these individuals (Jacobson, 2008).

This lack of clarity was illustrated graphically in research by Lyall et al (1995) and by McBrien and Murphy (2006), which found some reluctance among care staff to report crimes allegedly committed by people with intellectual (learning) disabilities. However, the seriousness of the offence is also a factor here: for example, in McBrien and Murphy's study '48% of care staff thought that theft should be reported, 68% thought assault should be reported, and 17% thought they would not report rape' (2006: 139) (Jacobson, 2008).

The arguments for people with learning disabilities being dealt with through the criminal justice system are influenced by a number of factors. The principle of inclusion of people with disabilities was enforced by the revision in 2005 of the DDA. This 'inclusion agenda' promotes the rights of people with disabilities to live full and active lives in society. As well as rights 'inclusion' brings with it certain duties – in this context the duty to live a law abiding life. Given the requirement in law for *mens rea* (or the intention to commit the crime, to be committed), if a person with learning disabilities is alleged to have committed an offence then he should be subject to the same due process as anyone else.

Another argument against diversion is that a person with learning disabilities who is alleged to have committed a crime may not appreciate the seriousness of his actions if it appears to him that he has been 'let off' by being diverted, and as a result he may go onto commit more serious offences (Murphy et al, forthcoming). A further compelling argument is that, as an alternative to criminal justice proceedings, a suspect with learning disabilities may be subject to compulsory treatment, for example under the Mental Health Act, without being afforded the opportunity to prove his innocence or knowing when he might be released (Seden, 2006).

The arguments for people with learning disabilities being diverted away from the criminal justice system tend to focus around three main areas:

- the probability that treatment in healthcare settings will be more effective
- the individual may remain known to services once treatment has ended
- the negative effect that a prison sentence is likely to have on an individual's general welfare and mental health while in prison and subsequently upon release.

In practice, there are few appropriate alternatives towards which a person with learning disabilities may be diverted and the question often asked is, 'diversion into what?'

There is also a lack of clarity on what action could, or should be taken if, for example, a person with learning disabilities is diverted away from the criminal justice system for treatment and absconds or fails to turn up for an appointment - should the individual be referred back to criminal justice?

In the spirit of 'inclusion', and given mens rea, people with learning disabilities who get into trouble with the police should be subject to the criminal justice process. However, prison today, in 2008, is not a realistic option for people with learning disabilities in particular. There are many reasons for this, the most fundamental being prison service non-compliance with the DDA (2005), and specifically the disability equality duty.

Sentencing for people with learning disabilities should therefore be limited to non-custodial options, for example a fine or a community sentence. If a fine is imposed, help with money management and budgeting should also be provided; if a community order is deemed appropriate, a person centred package of interventions and support should be made integral to the order. Where, due to the nature of the crime, only a custodial sentence is appropriate, diversion away from the criminal justice system should be considered.

The diversion of prisoners with mental health problems and learning disabilities is the subject of the Bradley review, see page 4. See also Jacobson (2008), (pages 5-8, 23-25).

7. Children with learning disabilities and difficulties and statutory education

What happens in school is important given the high correlation between educational attainment and employment, and poor educational attainment, school exclusion and offending behaviour. Prisoners with learning disabilities or difficulties in this study were three times as likely as those without such impairments to have been excluded from school, over half, which rose to almost two-thirds for those with possible learning disabilities . Children are not excluded from school because they have learning disabilities or difficulties – something else is happening.

Behaviour that leads a young person to being excluded from school may be the result of learning disabilities or difficulties that have gone unidentified and unsupported, resulting in problematic behaviour. Exclusion from school is likely to further reduce the chances of special educational need going unidentified (Loucks, 2007). Research by the British Dyslexia Association (BDA) showed that problematic behaviour in young people with dyslexia was evident early but was often identified before, or even instead of, the dyslexia. Over a third of the young prisoners the BDA were working with had a statement of special educational need for behavioural problems rather than for dyslexia (BDA, 2004).

Communication disorder is the most common disability seen in childhood and will affect many children with learning disabilities or difficulties. While speech and language therapy can help to remediate the disorder, the absence of such support has shown to lead to developmental disadvantage, poor social skills, behavioural problems, emotional difficulties and mental illness. In turn this can result in poor employment prospects, social exclusion and offending behaviour (Bryan and Mackenzie, 2008).

The Joint Inspection of Youth Offending Teams Annual Report, 2006/07, found that 62% of young people in contact with youth offending teams had 'schooling difficulties' and, in some cases, were unable to access services in the same way as other children in the locality.

A recent survey by Ofsted[49] into how well new teachers in England and Wales were prepared to teach pupils with learning disabilities and difficulties revealed that 'too much' initial teacher training 'was satisfactory rather than good', that there were considerable variations in practice and quality, and that there was a 'major weakness' in the monitoring of training. The report went onto say that 'in two thirds of the lessons taught by new and recently qualified teachers, provision for pupils with learning difficulties and/or disabilities was satisfactory or worse.'

While the extent to which problematic behaviour, leading to exclusion from school may be masking learning disabilities or difficulties is unclear, the relationship between exclusion and offending is well documented; as one prisoner in this study said:

> I was always causing trouble and getting sent out of classes. That was to cover myself for not being able to read and write.

Timely referrals and comprehensive assessments of any young person displaying problematic patterns of behaviour and appropriate packages of support should be provided before offending behaviour develops. Logic dictates that time and resources invested at this stage would pay dividends in the longer term.

Further research should be undertaken to explore the relationships between behavioural problems at school, effective identification of and support for children with learning disabilities and learning difficulties, and school exclusions.

Black and minority ethnic people with learning disabilities or difficulties who get into trouble with the police

Although there were a number of black and minority ethnic prisoners in this study, including smaller numbers of travellers, the likely effect of 'double discrimination' that many such people are likely to experience has not been specifically examined. This is an area where further research is required.

49. How well new teachers are prepared to teach pupils with learning difficulties and/or disabilities, September 2008

Concluding remarks:

The criminal justice system does not recognize, let alone meet, the particular needs of people who have learning disabilities or learning difficulties. From the point of arrest through to release from prison, the criminal justice system routinely fails them.

At worst, they are maltreated by the police, do not receive the support of an appropriate adult and don't fully understand what is happening to them. They may also incriminate themselves during police questioning. Once in court, their lack of understanding grows as their lives are taken over by opaque court procedures and legalistic terminology. In prison, although most understand why they are there, the process by which they arrived frequently remains a mystery. Typically, their situation in prison goes from bad to worse. Their inability to read and write very well, or at all and poor verbal comprehension skills relegates them to a shadowy world of not quite knowing what is going on around them or what is expected of them. They spend more time alone than their peers and have fewer things to do. They will have less contact with family and friends. They are more likely to experience high levels of depression and anxiety. They are more vulnerable to ridicule and exploitation. Many will be excluded from programmes to address their offending behaviour, which may mean longer in prison as a result.

At best, prisoners with learning disabilities or learning difficulties spoke about things in prison 'not being bad'. Some had got into trouble as a way to access support services or to get away from drink and drugs. One young offender said that it gave his family some respite and another said that he preferred prison; it was his 'family'. A number were pleased and even excited about having learnt to read and write while in prison, and one young offender said that coming to prison had done him good, he had learned a lot about himself and that the experience had made him a better person.

An underlying assumption of this study was that people with the most severe impairments were likely to be made the most vulnerable by the criminal justice process; that they would experience greater difficulties and would, as a result, cope less well than those with less severe impairments. Thus, the assumption was that offenders with learning disabilties were likley to fare less well in the criminal justice system than those with learning difficulties, and considerably less well than those with no such impairments.

While this proved generally accurate, there were some important deviations where prisoners with learning difficulties and low average IQ have coped less well.

This suggests that people with the most severe impairments, i.e. those with learning disabilities, are not uniformly made the most vulnerable by the different elements they encounter as they travel through the criminal justice system. Relying on labels, therefore, to determine levels of vulnerability and likely support needs becomes less helpful in this context. People with learning disabilities and learning difficulties are, in varying degrees, made vulnerable by the criminal justice process to which they are subject.

The discrimination experienced by prisoners with learning disabilities and learning difficulties across the criminal justice system is personal, systemic and routine.

Criminal justice agencies throughout the UK are failing in their legal duty to promote disability equality and to eliminate discrimination. In consequence the sense, if not the fact, of injustice prevails.

PRISONERS' VOICES   Part Three: Conclusion

Recommendations

Recommendations

The following recommendations reflect work undertaken over the last three years, including empirical research with prison staff and prisoners, reviews of relevant literature and policy, and extensive consultation with policy makers and practitioners, see appendix 8. Early recommendations published in reports from *No One Knows* have also been drawn upon. Members of the advisory group for *No One Knows* and members of the Working for Justice Group have been directly involved throughout the programme in both scoping the work and in shaping these recommendations.

These recommendations relate to the UK administrations and as such do not make nation specific references.

In addition to these recommendations, check lists that can be acted upon locally are included at appendix 9.

1. Disability discrimination and human rights

a. Criminal justice agencies should comply with the Disability Discrimination Act (2005) and specifically the Disability Equality Duty.

b. Individual prisons and courts should be brought into line with other public authorities and be required to produce their own Disability Equality Schemes.

c. All criminal justice agencies should undertake an audit of their services for compliance with ECHR rights, the Disability Discrimination Act (2005) and, specifically, the Disability Equality Duty; prisons and courts in particular should produce action plans demonstrating how they will ensure, and by when, that all services and provisions are fully accessible to people with learning disabilities and learning difficulties.

d. All criminal justice information, letters and forms should be in 'easy read'; all interventions should be accessible to offenders with learning disabilities or difficulties, or alternatives of the same quality provided.

e. The views of offenders with learning disabilities and learning difficulties should be sought on how well they perceive criminal justice agencies are meeting the Disability Equality Duty; the regularity for this should coincide with the production of the UK Justice Ministries' Disability Equality Schemes.

2. Knowing who has learning disabilities or difficulties

a. People with learning disabilities and learning difficulties should be identified at the point of arrest in order that appropriate support may be put into place and, where appropriate, the option to divert away from the criminal justice system considered; clear guidance and national standards for appropriate support and diversion at every stage of the criminal justice process are required.

b. The sharing of information between staff from criminal justice agencies, health, social services and education should be reciprocal, timely and effective, this is especially important with regard to criminal justice liaison and diversion; information sharing protocols and standards should be agreed, and information sharing monitored.

3. A needs led approach: collaborative multi-agency working

Local multi-agency 'forums'[50] , co-terminus with local authority areas, should fulfill the role of criminal justice liaison and diversion and develop local strategies for preventing offending and re-offending by people with learning disabilities and learning difficulties. Agencies involved in the forum should include: health (including specialist learning disability services), adult social services, children's services, housing, education and criminal justice,[51] and other relevant services, such as local disability partnership boards and appropriate adult networks. Forums should collaborate at a strategic level with other public authorities and service providers as necessary; information about the work of the forum should be published; participation in the forum should be mandatory for public authorities and an identified lead organization should be made accountable. The forum should be responsible for ensuring:

a. clear procedures for the referral of people considered vulnerable by criminal justice staff, for specialist attention and assessment

b. appropriate and routine support of people with learning disabilities and learning difficulties as they enter and travel through the criminal justice system; support should include advocacy

c. the development of a matrix of sentencing options and interventions, in particular community alternatives to custody and, for people with learning disabilities, alternatives to arrest; agencies should work together to develop interventions to maximize the range of options available; interventions should include person centered approaches to meeting support needs; the progress of individual offenders should be monitored

d. the effective resettlement of people with learning disabilities and learning difficulties on release from prison, including appropriate care packages such as support for independent living

e. regular multi-agency, multi-disciplinary training for forum members.

4. Workforce development

a. An 'equalities' agenda should be championed at a senior level within the UK Justice Ministries and all equalities should be given the same high level of priority.

b. Awareness training on learning disabilities and learning difficulties should be undertaken by all staff who come into contact with people as they enter and travel though the criminal justice system; people with learning disabilities and learning difficulties should be involved as co-trainers; a set of core materials should be developed and particular emphasis should be placed on effective communication.

c. Regular multi-agency, multi-disciplinary training should be undertaken, which should be the responsibility of local multi-agency forums.

d. Criminal justice staff should be encouraged to refer people they are concerned about to specialist services and be supported in their work with vulnerable people; clear referral procedures should be in place.

e. Prison healthcare should have ready access to learning disability expertise and speech and language therapy.

f. Mental health teams working within offender health should include learning disability expertise, including access to specialist learning disability services.

g. Education for prisoners, and offenders in the community, should include special education needs provision and learning support provided by appropriately qualified staff; provision should reflect the profile of the prisoner/offender population; there should be ready access to a dyslexia specialist.

h. Commissioners of health and social care services should work closely with local multi-agency forums to plan specialist services and provisions.

50. For example, analogous to criminal justice liaison and diversion schemes or multi-agency public protection arrangements.
51. Including police, courts, probation, youth offending services and prisons.

5. Alternatives to custody

Community sentences, as an alternative to custody, should be used for offenders with learning disabilities in particular and for offenders with learning difficulties wherever possible, for example for low level crimes and where there is no risk to the public.

6. National standards

There should be national standards for health and social care provision, including clear guidance and accountability for transition arrangements between children's and adult services; eligibility criteria for support should be flexible and inclusive, and should not be used to exclude people and to ration services; people who offend should not be denied access to services on the basis of their offending behaviour or because they have previously been an offender.

7. Clarification

a. There should be national guidelines on methods and criteria for the assessment of fitness for police interview by healthcare professionals. (Jacobson, 2008).

b. The concept of criminal responsibility appears unclear when applied to people with learning disabilities. Guidance is required on the circumstances that should prompt learning disability services and specialist care services to bring an incident to the attention of the police and on the factors which make it appropriate for an individual to be diverted from the criminal justice system to specialist health services (Jacobson, 2008).

8. Terminology

Greater precision in terminology is required to avoid confusion and to ensure people receive appropriate support. Current terminology tends to conflate learning disability with mental illness – in referring, for example to suspects who are 'mentally disordered or otherwise mentally vulnerable' (Jacobson, 2008), while 'vulnerable' has a very different meaning in prison to that used by the police. In prison, 'vulnerable' is routinely used to describe the threats posed to certain prisoners, rendering them 'vulnerable', due to the nature of their offending, for example prisoners who are sex offenders; at the police station the term 'vulnerable' is used to describe people less able to cope with the rigors of police caution and interview and who are in need of support.

PRISONERS' VOICES

Appendices

PRISONERS'VOICES   Appendix 1

Reports and publications from *No One Knows,* in date order:

- Prisoners with learning difficulties and learning disabilities – review of prevalence and associated needs. Loucks, N. (2006), PDF.

- Easy read introduction to the work of the Prison Reform Trust and the *No One Knows* programme. Working for Justice Group with Talbot, J.

- Identifying and supporting prisoners with learning difficulties and learning disabilities: the views of prison staff. Talbot, J. (2007).

- Briefing paper: Prisoners with learning difficulties and learning disabilities – review of prevalence and associated needs. Loucks, N. (2007).

- Briefing paper: Human rights and offenders with learning difficulties and learning disabilities. Watson, J. (2007), PDF.

- Identifying and supporting prisoners with learning difficulties and learning disabilities: the views of prison staff in Scotland. Loucks, N. (2007).

- Police responses to suspects with learning disabilities and learning difficulties: a review of policy and practice. Jacobson, J (2008).

- Identifying and supporting prisoners with learning difficulties and learning disabilities: the views of prison staff in Northern Ireland. Loucks, N. (2008).

- A review of court provision for defendants with learning disabilities and learning difficulties. Jacobson, J. with Seden, R. (forthcoming).

  All publications are available from the Prison Reform Trust and PDFs can be found at www.prisonreformtrust.org.uk/nok

Appendix 2

Membership of the Working for Justice Group

- Tom Bromley
- Steven Dean
- Anthony Fletcher
- Darron Heads
- Graham Keeton
- Michelle Law
- Danny McDowell
- William Morris
- Mark Ogilvie
- Lee Owen
- Michael Wall
- Carl[52]
- Andrew

Apart from Lee, all Working for Justice Group members were invited to participate by KeyRing Living Support Networks and are network members. Lee was invited by the Avon Forensic Community Learning Disability Team and was supported by Cintre Community.

Appendix 3

Membership of the advisory group

- Chair: the Rt Hon. The Baroness Joyce Quin
- Alan Bicknell, Regional Co-ordinator, The National Autistic Society
- Professor Karen Bryan, University of Surrey, Faculty of Health and Medical Sciences
- Judy Clements, London and South East, Independent Police Complaints Commission (2006/07)
- Shirley Cramer, Chief Executive, Dyslexia Action
- Dr Kimmett Edgar, Head of Research, Prison Reform Trust
- Dr Andrew Fraser, Director of Health and Care, Scottish Prison Service
- Dr Ann Hagell, Freelance Research Associate, Policy Research Bureau and PRT trustee
- Brian Ingram, Head of Resettlement, Northern Ireland Prison Service (2006/07)
- Dr Glyn Jones, Consultant Psychiatrist, Learning Disability Directorate, Abertawe Bro Morgannwg University NHS Trust
- Linda Jones, Head of Partnerships and Alliances, Office of the South East Regional Offender Manager
- Janice McHenry, Learning and Skills Adviser, Northern Ireland Prison Service, from 2007
- Glynis Murphy, Professor of Clinical Psychology of Learning Disability, Tizard Centre, University of Kent
- Robert Newman, Director: education, training and employment, Youth Justice Board (2006/07)
- Sue O'Hara, Head of Offender Learning, Learning and Skills Council
- Sarah Payne, Regional Offender Manager (South East), National Offender Management Service
- Tom Robson, National Executive, Prison Officer Association
- James Shanley, Governor, HMP Birmingham
- Keith Smith, Chief Executive, British Institute of Learning Disabilities
- Kathryn Stone, Chief Executive, Voice UK
- Jo Williams, Chief Executive, Mencap

52. Carl and Andrew were early members of the group and as it has not been possible to secure their permission to include their surnames in this report, only their first name has been used.

Appendix 4

Some common characteristics of people with learning disabilities, learning difficulties and people on the autistic spectrum

Learning disabilities

People with learning disabilities, also referred to as intellectual disabilities, are likely to have limited language ability, comprehension and communication skills, which might mean they have difficulty understanding and responding to questions; they may have difficulty recalling information and take longer to process information; they may be acquiescent and suggestible (Clare, 2003) and, under pressure, may try to appease other people (Home Office Research Findings, 44).

Most people with learning disabilities have greater health needs than the rest of the population: they are more likely to experience mental illness and are more prone to chronic health problems, epilepsy, and physical and sensory disabilities. (Valuing People, 2001; Rickford and Edgar, 2005). Further, the health needs of people with learning disabilities are often not adequately addressed.

People with learning disabilities living in private households are much more likely to live in areas characterized by high levels of social deprivation; they are also much more likely to experience material and social hardship than people with learning disabilities in supported accommodation services (Emerson and Hatton, 2008).

Learning difficulties

Specific learning difficulties, of which dyslexia is the most common, cover a range of impairments including dyspraxia, dyscalculia, attention deficit disorder (ADD) and attention deficit hyperactivity disorder (ADHD).

Dyslexia is a developmental difficulty that is characterised by phonological deficits, the skill that underlies the acquisition of literacy; it occurs regardless of intelligence levels. People with dyslexia often have 'unexpected' difficulties in learning to read and write and read hesitantly; they may misread certain words, which makes understanding difficult; they may have difficulty with sequencing, for example getting dates in order; they may have poor organisation and time management skills and difficulties organising their thoughts clearly. The number, type and characteristics of dyslexia vary from one dyslexic person to another and individuals can be mildly, moderately or severely affected. The incidence of dyslexia in the general population is 10%, with 6% being slightly affected and 4% having more severe difficulties; in every school classroom two to three children will be affected.

Dyspraxia causes difficulties in coordination and those affected often have poor handwriting and motor control. Dyscalculia refers to difficulties with maths.

Attention deficit disorder (ADD) and attention deficit hyperactivity disorder (ADHD) refers to a range of behaviours associated with poor attention span. These may include impulsiveness, restlessness and hyperactivity, as well as inattentiveness, and often prevent children from learning and socializing well.

Characteristics associated with attention deficit disorder include failing to pay close attention to detail, failure to finish tasks or to sustain attention in activities, seeming not to listen to what is said, not following through instructions, being disorganized about tasks and activities, easily distracted, and forgetful in the course of daily activities.

Characteristics associated with hyperactivity and impulsivity include: fidgeting with hands or feet, blurting out answers before the questions have been completed, failure to wait in line or not waiting turns in group situations, interrupting or intruding on others, for example butting into the conversations of others, and talking excessively without appropriate response to social restraint.

About 1.7% of the UK population, mostly children, have ADD or ADHD. Boys are more likely to be affected.

Many individuals with specific learning difficulties have characteristics in all the areas of difficulty, which means that assessing their specific needs is very important for planning help and support. Specific learning difficulties that are not identified or dealt with at an early age can cause significant life problems, particularly when the family is already socially disadvantaged.

Autism Spectrum Disorder

Autism Spectrum Disorder (ASD) is the term used to describe a range of life long neurodevelopmental conditions affecting social understanding and behaviour, communication and functioning. Additionally, such individuals commonly show a rigid, repetitive or restricted repertoire of behaviours or intense narrow interests. Often these will be in subjects or topics where they may be exceptionally knowledgeable and may sometimes get them into trouble, such as computer hacking.

Superficially good language may mask underlying difficulties of comprehension together with an instinctive inability to understand how other people think and act. This leads to inappropriate responses in social situations, which are commonly misinterpreted as rudeness, contrariness or worse. Consequently they may have great difficulty in maintaining social relationships, especially with peers or those in authority.

Their apparently odd social demeanor and interaction with others may also place them at risk of being bullied. Individuals with these conditions are of all levels of intelligence and functioning but it is those with Asperger syndrome who may be at higher risk of entering the criminal justice system. They may be suggestible or respond literally to rules or to questions.

Other medical conditions related to anxiety, depression and attention deficit type or mood disorders are also much more common in these individuals. (Thanks to Richard Mills for this section on ASD).

Together, people with learning disabilities or difficulties and people on the autistic spectrum represent some of the most vulnerable people in the offender population.

Appendix 5

LIPS screening tool

The LIPS screening tool was designed to identify prisoners on probation in the bottom 5% of the IQ range and was developed by Jon Mason[53].

By their very nature, screening tools used to identify the likelihood of learning disabilities will have an intrinsic risk of under and over identification of the population screened, for example the tool will fail to identify some people who do have learning disabilities and will identify others who may not. A validity study for the LIPS screening tool identified good sensitivity with 87% of cases correctly classified.

The LIPS screening tool is in four parts:

- parts 1 and 2 assess cognitive skills using verbal and non-verbal assessment techniques. The verbal assessment technique used was an adapted version of the Quick Test (QT)[54] and the non-verbal was the Clock Drawing Test (CDT)[55]
- part 3 comprises six questions related to social functioning skills
- part 4 comprises five questions relating to other predictors of learning disabilities, for example contact with services, attendance at a special school.

In order to screen 'positive', i.e. a diagnosis of learning disability is probable, those undertaking the screen must score less than a given number for both the Quick Test (QT) and the Clock Drawing Test (CDT). In addition certain responses relating to social functioning skills (Part 3) and other predictors of learning disabilities are required (Part 4). The accumulation of these factors will determine whether a learning disability is probable or not. By slightly increasing the QT score cut off, but leaving the CDT score and other requirements (Parts 3 and 4) the same, it is also possible to determine the probability of borderline learning disabilities and a low average IQ.

It is also possible to draw certain inferences where those undertaking LIPS score less than a given number on either the QT or the CDT, see appendix 7.

Quick Test scores:
For learning disability the QT cut-off was 30 or less; for borderline learning disabilities, 31 or 32, and for low average IQ, 33 – 37.

Clock Drawing Test Score:
For learning disability, borderline learning disability and low average IQ the CDT cut-off was 13 or less.

---

53. See Mason, J. & Murphy, G.H. (2002)
54. Ammons and Ammons, 1962
55. Freedman et al, 1994

Appendix 6

Research team:

- Will Antell, PRT research associate and former group manager for offender learning, Strode College (conducted interviews at two of the ten prisons in England and Wales)

- Julia Braggins, PRT research associate (conducted interviews at two of the ten prisons in England and Wales)

- Francesca Cooney, PRT (conducted interviews at one of the ten prisons in England and Wales)

- Karen Bryan, professor of clinical practice, Faculty of Health and Medical Sciences, University of Surrey and advisory group member for *No One Knows* (conducted interviews at two of the ten prisons in England and Wales)

- Vicki Herrington, independent researcher and PRT volunteer (conducted interviews at one of the ten prisons in England and Wales)

- Dr Nancy Loucks, independent criminologist and PRT research associate (conducted interviews at the four Scottish prisons)

- Glynis Murphy, professor of clinical psychology, Tizard Centre, University of Kent and advisory group member for *No One Knows* (conducted interviews at four of the ten prisons in England and Wales)

- Jenny Talbot, programme manager, *No One Knows,* PRT (research manager; conducted interviews at eight of the ten prisons in England and Wales)

Appendix 7

Profile of prisoners interviewed[56]

Gender: 14% of all prisoners were women compared to 6% of the prison population for England and Wales and 5% for Scotland, as at June 2006

Age: the average age of all prisoners was 32 years compared to 30 years for the prison population in England and Wales and 32 years in Scotland.

Ethnicity: table 6 shows the ethnicity of prisoners interviewed compared to prison populations in England and Wales and in Scotland.

Table 6: ethnicity of prisoners interviewed compared to prison populations in England and Wales, and Scotland

	Prisoners interviewed	Prison population, England & Wales	Prison population, Scotland
White	77% (133)	73%	97%
Black	10% (17)	15%	1%
Asian	4% (7)	7%	2%
Mixed race	3% (5)	3%	0.1%
Other	0.5% (1)	1%	0.3%
Data missing	6% (10)		

The status of prisoners interviewed, for example whether sentenced or on remand, compared to prison populations in England and Wales and in Scotland, is shown at table 7.

Table 7: status of prisoners interviewed

	Target group	Comparison group	Prison population, England & Wales	Prison population, Scotland
Remand/untried	14%	11%	18%	22%
Sentenced	77%	74%	81%	78%
Other	8%	16%	1%	0%
Interviewee doesn't know	1%	0%	n/a	n/a

LIPS screening tool:
The majority of prisoners referred by prison staff were assessed using the LIPS and it identified 27 prisoners where there was a possibility of learning disabilities, and seven where there was a possibility of borderline learning disabilities[57]. A further 25 prisoners were identified as possibly being of low average IQ[58].

56. Prison service statistics taken from: Ministry of Justice statistical bulletin, offender management caseload statistics 2006 (December 2007) and Scottish Government statistical bulletin, crime and justice series, prison statistics, Scotland 2006/07.
57. IQ range 70 – 79 plus diminished adaptive ability, see WHO definition, page 2.
58. IQ range 80 – 89 plus diminished adaptive ability, see WHO definition, page 2.

The results of the LIPS quick test (QT) and clock drawing test (CDT) are shown at tables 8 and 9 below.

- Quick Test: for possible learning disabilities the QT cut-off used was 30 or less; for possible borderline learning disabilities, 31 to 32, and for possible 'low average', 33 to 37

- Clock Drawing Test: for possible learning disabilities, borderline learning disabilities and 'low average' the CDT cut-off used was 13 or less

Table 8:

Quick Test (QT)				
	Minimum score	Maximum score	Mean	Standard deviation
Target group (n = 145)	8	46	31.61	6.615
Comparison group (n = 18)	32	46	38.33	4.116
Possible LD or BLD[59] (n = 34)	8	32	26.53	5.148
The results between the target and comparison groups were highly significant: t = 4.2; p <0.001				

Table 9:

Clock drawing test (CDT)				
	Minimum score	Maximum score	Mean	Standard deviation
Target group (n = 139)	4	15	12.81	2.296
Comparison group (n = 18)	9	15	13.61	2.033
Possible LD or BLD[60] (n = 34)	4	13	10.76	2.203
The results between the target and comparison groups were not significant				

In addition to the 34 prisoners with learning disabilities and borderline learning disabilities, a further 33 prisoners scored 30 or less on the QT and 40 scored 13 or less on the CDT[61]. Although, according to the LIPS, none of this group were likely to have learning disabilities (because the accumulation of scores required for parts 1-4 of the LIPS hadn't been realized), such low scores in either the QT or the CDT means that prisoners will experience difficulties with verbal comprehension skills, including difficulties understanding certain words and in expressing themselves.

Of those prisoners identified by LIPS as having possible learning or borderline learning disabilities almost half (47%) were also identified by prison staff as having learning disabilities. However, at least one interviewee who was not identified by the LIPS had a diagnosis of learning disability confirmed by healthcare.

See appendix 5 for further details about the LIPS screening tool.

59. Learning disabilities or borderline learning disabilities (note: the 34 possible LD or BLD are part of the target group)
60. ibid
61. Note: on its own a low CDT score may also suggest a previous head injury, specific difficulties with non-verbal abilities and dyspraxia, but further investigation would be necessary before any conclusions may be drawn.

Appendix 8

No One Knows Consultation June 2008

The following people took part in a consultation event in June 2008 that informed the concluding discussion and recommendations contained in this report; I am very grateful for their help. Their inclusion on this list does not mean they agree with everything written in this report.

Name	Organisation
Abernethy, Rosemary	London Probation
Ainsworth, Michael	Ministry of Justice
Andrews, Ruth	Northgate and Prudhoe NHS Trust
Armstrong, Allison	Northgate hospital
Ashworth, Pam	HMP Wakefield
Aubrey, Tony	Association of Chief Police Officers & Metropolitan Police
Baldwin, Debra	NOMS
Badmus, Ami	Home Office
Bell, Gillian	Northumberland, Tyne & Wear Trust
Berry, Jan	Immediate past chairman, Police Federation
Boer, Harm	Janet Shaw Clinic
Bowles, Elizabeth	EHRC
Boyd, Steven	St Helen's Council
Braggins, Julia	PRT research associate
Bryan, Karen	University of Surrey, professor of clinical practice
Cannings, Carrie	Ministry of Justice
Cantrell, Helen	HM Prison Service
Clare, Isabel	University of Cambridge
Clayton, Susan	HMP&YOI Chelmsford
Cobb, Janet	Foundation for People with Learning Disabilities
Cramer, Shirley	Dyslexia Action, chief executive
Curen, Richard	Respond
Curtis, Neil	Home Office
Dale, Colin	UCLAN
David, Siriol	HM Prison Service
Dean, Janet	Norfolk County Council
Degg, Sharon	HMYOI Ashfield
Dunning, Norman	Enable Scotland
Edgar, Kimmett	PRT, head of research
Eisenstadt, Naomi	Social Exclusion Taskforce, Director
Erne, Maureen	NIPS
Farmer, Jenny	Magistrates Association
Fitzpatrick, Monica	NIPS
Flaxington, Frances	NOMS
Fraser, Andrew	SPS, Director of health and social care
Freeman, Mark	Department of Health, offender health
Gemmell, Linda	HMP Gartree
Giannasi, Paul	Home Office
Gibbs, Penelope	PRT, strategy to reduce child/youth imprisonment

Appendix 8

Giraud-Saunders, Alison	Foundation for People with LD
Greatrex, Edward	OLSU
Green, Jan	HMYOI Polmont
Greig, Rob	National Development Team
Gyford, Rachel	London Probation
Hadley, Lorna	YOT manager, Newham,
Haines, Jo	
Hames, Anne-Marie	HMP & YOI Parc
Hammerton, Steve	HMP & YOI Holloway
Hammond, Tracy	KeyRing
Hart, Di	National Children's Bureau
Hende, Robin van den	Voice UK, Respond, Ann Craft Trust
Hepworth, Karina	Kirklees YOT
Hillman, Jocelyn	Working Chance CIC
Holland, Tony	University of Cambridge
Israr, Mo	HMP Wakefield
Iyer, Anu	St Andrew's Healthcare
Jacobson, Jessica	Independent criminologist
Jameson, Kathleen	EHRC
Jenkin, Jen	Northgate& Prudhoe NHS Trust
Jones, Glyn	Abertawe Bro Morgannwg University NHS Trust
Jones, Pat	Prisoners' Education Trust
Keys, Duncan	POA
Khan, Lorraine	Sainsbury Centre for mental health
Kirkpatrick, Karyn	KeyRing
Lawrence-Parr, Carole	Dorset PCT
Leigh, Liz	HMP Rye Hill
Loucks, Nancy	Independent criminologist
Lowe, Trevor	Ministry of Justice
Lynam, Jane	Justice's Clerk's Society
Lyon, Juliet	PRT
Mackenzie, Jane	RCSLT
Martin, Neill	NOMS (Hull Probation)
McAleenan, Dawn	NACRO
McArdle, Theresa	
McHenry, Janice	NIPS, Learning and Skills Adviser
McKinnon, Iain	Newcastle University
McLeod, Anita	NOMS
McPhee, Chris	HMP & YOI Hull
Miller, Rachel	NIPS
Mills, Richard	The National Autistic Society
Minnitt, Diz	Association YOT managers
Mitchell, Merron	Manchester college
Moore, Julia	Devon & Cornwall Constabulary

Morton, Glynis	TDI
Murphy, Glynis	University of Kent
Narducci, Wendy	Norfolk AA scheme
Narey, Abby	HMP & YOI Holloway
O'Brien, Greg	Northumberland, Tyne & Wear NHS Trust; University of Northumbria
O'Dwyer, Patrick	NOMS London
O'Hara, Sue	LSC, head of offender learning
O'Meara, Tricia	Lincolnshire Probation
Ormerod, Pamela	Magistrates Association
Owers, Anne	HM Inspectorate of Prisons, chief inspector
Panrucker, Colin	HMP Bronzefield
Payne, Sarah	NOMS, South East ROM
Pearson, Alan	Northumbria Police
Perry, Joanna	CPS
Piper, Dean	Welsh Assembly Government
Podmore, John	Offender Health
Poynter, Jo	Valuing People Support Team
Pritchard, Lis	NAAN
Quin, Joyce	House of Lords
Radford, Alan	HMP Edmunds Hill
Rickford, Dora	PRT research associate & NOK evaluator
Saunders, Chris	HMP & YOI Holloway
Shanley, James	HMP Birmingham, governor
Sharples, Sue	HMP Leyhill
Shew, Helen	HMP Wakefield
Skinns, Layla	Institute for criminal policy research
Smith, Keith	British Institute of Learning Disabilities, chief executive
Smith, Kevin	NPIA
Stevens, Roger	NOMS
Stone, Kathryn	Voice UK, chief executive
Stubbs, Marion	Ministry of Justice
Talbot, Jenny	PRT
Tancred, Tania	Kent Probation Area
Thomas, Glyn	HM Court Services
Thornton, Paul	Northumberland Tyne and Wear NHS Trust
Treharne, Mike	HMP & YOI Parc
Vaughan, Richard	YJB
Ward, Richard	OLSU
Weightman, John	IMB
Whetstone, Christine	IMB, HMP & YOI Holloway
Williams, Fiona	Rainsbrook STC
Williams, Michael	Judicial studies board
Williams, Rowena	NHS Wales
Winters, Lucia	Council for disabled children
Wright, John	HM Court Services
Younis, Nargis	NACRO

Appendix 9

Checklists

These checklists for action[62] will help to ensure that people with learning disabilities or difficulties are identified and their needs met as they enter and travel through the criminal justice system; they are not exhaustive and professionals and practitioners will no doubt identify more that can be done.

POLICE			
	Yes	No	Action
Is there a way of screening people brought in for questioning to identify possible learning disabilities or difficulties?			
Is information for police suspects and detainees accessible, for example 'easy read'?			
When suspects are identified as possibly having learning disabilities or difficulties do you ensure they understand their rights, in particular the right to legal advice?			
When suspects are identified as possibly having learning disabilities or difficulties do you obtain an Appropriate Adult (AA)?			
Is there an AA training scheme in your area and are AAs easy to get in relatively a short time?			
Are police personnel trained in how to interview people with learning disabilities or difficulties?			
Are there good links with local adult social services and learning disability services and a named person to contact when a suspect has a learning disability?			
Do police officers undertake awareness training on learning disabilities/difficulties?			
Are copies of *Positive Practice Positive Outcomes* readily available?			

62. Apart from the checklist for LDPBs, which was developed by Mike Cleasby (Learning Disabilities Team at Darlington Borough Council), these checklists have been adapted from *'Breaking the Cycle. Better help for people with learning disabilities at risk of committing offences: A framework for the North West.'* (Murphy, 2006)

Checklists

COURTS:			
	Yes	No	Action
Is the court informed when a defendant has learning disabilities or difficulties?			
Does the court have access to a criminal justice liaison and diversion scheme with learning disability expertise?			
Is information for defendants accessible, for example 'easy read'?			
Does the court adapt its procedures for people with learning disabilities or difficulties, for example, questioning styles and support with communication? How does the court ensure that defendants with learning disabilities or difficulties understand what is happening?			
Is the court aware of local service provision for people with learning disabilities that could be made part of a community order?			
Do court personnel undertake awareness training on learning disabilities/difficulties?			
Are copies of *Positive Practice Positive Outcomes* readily available?			

Checklists

PRISON:			
	Yes	No	Action
Is there a way of screening people to identify possible learning disabilities or difficulties on arrival into prison?			
Are information sharing protocols in place, including with healthcare and education, to ensure that appropriate information is shared for the benefit of the prisoner?			
Is prison information and are prison forms accessible, for example 'easy read'?			
Are arrangements in place to support prisoners unable to read and/or write?			
Is the prison regime accessible to all prisoners?			
Are adapted accredited cognitive skills programmes available?			
Are there good links with local adult social services and learning disability services?			
Are adult social services alerted at least 12 weeks in advance prior to a prisoner with learning disabilities leaving prison?			
Do prison staff undertake awareness training on learning disabilities/difficulties?			
Are there good links with your local Learning Disability Partnership Board?			
Prisoner learning: are staff qualified in special education needs and does provision match the population profile of prisoners? Do staff have ready access to a dyslexia specialist?			

continued

Checklists

PRISON:			
	Yes	No	Action
Prisoner learning: are shared strategies in place with prison staff to help prisoners unable to read and write very well to cope better with reading prison information and filling in prison forms?			
Prisoner healthcare: are there good links with local learning disability services and a named person to contact?			
Prisoner healthcare: do healthcare staff work with prison officers to meet support needs of prisoners with learning disabilities?			
Prisoner healthcare: Do you have learning disability nurses/in reach learning disability nurses?			
Prisoner healthcare: are staff aware of the factors that might lead to a prisoner being 'diverted' into specialist healthcare and what procedures should be followed?			
Are copies of *Positive Practice Positive Outcomes* readily available?			

Checklists

Appendix 9

PROBATION:			
	Yes	No	Action
Do you have a system of screening to find out which of your clients have learning disabilities or learning difficulties?			
Do you have effective information sharing protocols in place?			
Is information accessible, for example 'easy read'?			
What arrangements have you made for clients unable to read any written information or to write?			
Are adapted accredited cognitive skills programmes available?			
Are there good links with your local community learning disability service for help with clients with learning disabilities?			
Do probation staff undertake awareness training on learning disabilities/difficulties?			
Offender learning: are assessment procedures, inclusive learning and additional learning support readily available?			
Are there good links with your local Learning Disability Partnership Board?			
What action has been/is being undertaken to ensure that all activities and opportunities are accessible to all clients?			
Are copies of *Positive Practice Positive Outcomes* readily available?			

Checklists

LEARNING DISABILITY PARTNERSHIP BOARDS (LDPB):			
	Yes	No	Action
Has the LDPB allocated a liaison person for their local prison(s)? This person can signpost prison staff to local support services and offer advice on things such as 'easy read'			
Has the LDPB allocated a liaison person for their local probation service? This person can signpost prison staff to local support services and offer advice on things such as 'easy read'			
Does the LDPB offer advice and guidance on advocacy?			
Does the LDPB/forensic services offer support to prison staff working with prisoners with learning disabilities?			
Does the LDPB support prison staff with learning disability awareness training, including person centred approaches to providing support?			
Does the LDPB know who the PCT lead is for the healthcare of people with learning disabilities in prison?			
Does the LDPB work with prison healthcare to ensure that prisoners with learning disabilities receive health checks and information about medical conditions, maintaining good health and how to access healthcare in prison?			
Does the LDPB work with prisons to support people with learning disabilities as they prepare to leave prison, for example with employment, training and housing, to ensure a smooth transition?			
Does the LDPB offer a befriending service to people with learning disabilities on their release from prison?			

Appendix 10

References:

Ammons, R B, and Ammons, C H (1962) 'The Quick Test (QT): Provisional manual,' Psychological Reports, 11, pages 111-161.

Bromley Briefings, Prison Factfile (June, 2008) Prison Reform Trust: London.

British Dyslexia Association (2004) Unrecognised Dyslexia and the Route to Offending.
Report of a project between the British Dyslexia Association and Bradford Youth Offending Team. Reading: British Dyslexia Association.

British Educational Research Association (2004) Revised ethical guidelines for educational research (2004), online: http://www.bera.ac.uk/publications/pdfs/ETHICA1.PDF

Bryan, K. (2004) Preliminary study of the prevalence of speech and language difficulties in young offenders. International Journal of Language and Communication Disorders 39(3), 391-400.

Bryan, K., Freer, J., and Furlong, C. (2004) Speech and Language Therapy for Young People in Prison Project: Third Project Report, May 2004 – October 2004, University of Surrey.

Bryan, K., Mackenzie, J. (2008) Meeting the speech, language and communication needs of vulnerable young people: model of service delivery for those at risk of offending and re-offending: Royal College of Speech and Language Therapists.

Clare, I.C.H. (2003) Psychological vulnerabilities of adults with mild learning disabilities: implications for suspects during police detention and interviewing, unpublished PhD thesis, Institute of Psychiatry, King's College, London.

Clare, I. C. H. and Gudjonsson, G. H. (1991) "Recall and understanding of the caution and 44 rights in police detention among persons of average intellectual ability and persons with a mental handicap, Proceedings of the First DCLP Annual Conference 1, 34-42, Leicester: British Psychological Society (Issues in Criminological and Legal Psychology Series, No. 17).

Department of Health (2001) Valuing People. White Paper, Cm 5086. London: Department of Health.

Department of Health (2007) Improving Health, Supporting Justice. London: Department of Health.

Edgar, K., Rickford, R., Talbot, J. (2008) Getting health and community care to prisoners who will need it on release, Prison Service Journal, September 2008, No 179.

Emerson, E. and Hatton, C. (2008) 'People with Learning Disabilities in England'. CeDR, Lancaster University, UK.

Freedman, M., Leach, L., Kaplan, E., Winocur, G., Shulman, K. I., Delis, D. C. (1994) Clock Drawing:
A Neuropsychological Analysis, USA: Oxford University Press.

HM Chief Inspectors of Prisons and Probation (2008). The indeterminate sentence for public protection;
A thematic review, London: HMCIP.

HM Treasury (2007) PSA Delivery Agreement 16: increase the proportion of socially excluded adults in settled accommodation and employment, education or training.

Hare D., Gould J., Mills R., and Wing L. (1996) A preliminary study of autistic disorders in the three special hospitals of England: NAS.

Harrington, R. and Bailey, S., with Chitsabesan, P., Kroll, L., Macdonald, W., Sneider, S., Kenning, C., Taylor, G.,

Appendix 10

Byford, S., and Barrett, B. (2005) Mental Health Needs and Effectiveness of Provision for Young Offenders in Custody and in the Community, London: Youth Justice Board for England and Wales.

Health Service Journal (2008) Prison Healthcare: community spirit and honour among thieves, 18 September 2008, Tabreham, J.

Home Office (1990) Provision for Mentally Disordered Offenders, Circular 66/90, London: Home Office.

Home Office (1996) Research Findings, No. 44 Witnesses with Learning Disabilities: London: Home Office.

Humber, E., Snow P.C. (2001) The language processing and production skills of juvenile offenders: a pilot investigation, Psychiatry, Psychology and Law: 1-11.

Ireland, J. (2002) Bullying in Prisons, The Psychologist, 15, (3), pp 130-133.

Jacobson, J. (2008) Police responses to suspects with learning disabilities and learning difficulties: a review of policy and practice. London: Prison Reform Trust.

Jacobson, J. with Seden, R. (forthcoming) A review of court provision for defendants with learning disabilities and learning difficulties. London: Prison Reform Trust.

Joint Committee on Human Rights (2008) A life like any other? Human Rights of Adults with Learning Disabilities. Seventh Report of Session 2007-08. London: TSO.

Joint Inspection of Youth Offending Teams Annual Report, 2006/07; HMI Probation.

Jones, L. J. (2008) Access to Prison Regimes for Prisoners with Learning Difficulties and Disabilities. Unpublished thesis in part fulfillment of MSt in Applied, Penology and Management. University of Cambridge.

Liebling, A. (1992) Suicides in Prison. London: Routledge.

Loucks, N. (2007) Prisoners with learning difficulties and learning disabilities – review of prevalence and associated needs. London: Prison Reform Trust.

Loucks, N. (2007) Identifying and supporting prisoners with learning difficulties and learning disabilities: the views of prison staff in Scotland. London: Prison Reform Trust.

Lyall, I., Holland, A. J., Collins, S. (1995) Offending by adults with learning disabilities: identifying need in one health district, Mental Handicap Research 8, 99-109.

McBrien, J. (2003) The Intellectually Disabled Offender: Methodological Problems in Identification, Journal of Applied Research in Intellectual Disabilities 16.

McBrien, J. and Murphy, G. (2006) Police and carers' views on reporting alleged offences by people with intellectual disabilities, Psychology, Crime & Law 12(2), 127-144.

Mason, J. and Murphy, G. H. (2002) Intellectual disability amongst people on probation: prevalence and outcome, Journal of Intellectual Disability Research 46(3), 230-238.

Mottram, P. G. (2007) HMP Liverpool, Styal and Hindley Study Report. Liverpool: University of Liverpool.

Murphy, G. (2006) Breaking the Cycle. Better help for people with learning disabilities at risk of committing offences: A framework for the North West.

Murphy, G., and Mason, J. (2005) People with Intellectual Disabilities who are At Risk of Offendin, In N. Bouras, ed., Psychiatric and Behavioural Disorders in Developmental Disabilities and Mental Retardation, Cambridge: Cambridge University Press.

Appendix 10

NACRO: Findings of the 2004 survey of Court Diversion/Criminal Justice Mental Health Liaison Schemes for mentally disordered offenders in England and Wales, March 2005, NACRO.

Ofsted (2008) (reference number: 070223) How well new teachers are prepared to teach pupils with learning difficulties and/or disabilities, London: Ofsted.

PRT briefing (2007) Indefinitely maybe? How the indeterminate sentence for public protection is unjust and unsustainable, London, Prison Reform Trust.

PRT briefing (2007) Watson, J. Human rights and offenders with learning difficulties and learning disabilities.

PRT briefing (2008) Titan Prison: a gigantic mistake. London, Prison Reform Trust.

PRT submission to the Joint Committee on Human Rights, The Human Rights of Adults with Learning Disabilities, call for evidence, June 2007.

Prison Service (England and Wales) (2008) PSO 2855, Prisoners with Disabilities.

Prison Service (England and Wales) (2007) PSO 2750, Violence Reduction.

Prison Service (England and Wales) (2004) PSO 0100, The Prison Rules 1999.

Prison Service Journal (2008) Getting Healthcare, Housing Support, and Community Care set up for prisoners who will need it on release, No 179, September 2008, Edgar, K., Rickford, D., Talbot, J.

PSA Delivery Agreement 16: Increase the proportion of socially excluded adults in settled accommodation and employment, education or training; October 2007, HM Government, HM Treasury.

Rack, J. (2005) The Incidence of Hidden Disabilities in the Prison Population, Egham, Surrey: Dyslexia Institute.

Reed Review of Services for Mentally Disordered Offenders and others requiring similar services - People with learning disabilities (mental Handicap) or with autism' (Department of Health and Home Office 1992) HMSO.

Rickford, D. and Edgar, K. (2005) Troubled Inside: Responding to the Mental Health Needs of Men in Prison. London: Prison Reform Trust.

Robson, C (1993) Real World Research: A resource for social scientists and practitioner-researchers, Blackwell.

Scottish Prison Service rules: Prisons and Young Offenders Institutions (Scotland) Rules 1994: http://www.sps.gov.uk//Default.aspx?DocumentID=430c105d-b1b0-49e0-b026-2fd5d61b46a5

Seden, R. (2006) Access to Justice for Vulnerable Defendants, monthly journal of the Legal Action Group, March 2006.

Silicon.com: Prisoners phone bills too high says watchdog, 23 September 2008: http://www.silicon.com/publicsector/0,3800010403,39292540,00.htm

Social Exclusion Unit (2002) Reducing re-offending by ex-prisoners, London: Office of the Deputy Prime Minister.

Tabreham, J. (18 September 2008) Prison Healthcare: community spirit and honour among thieves, Health Service Journal.

Talbot, J. (2007) Identifying and supporting prisoners with learning difficulties and learning disabilities: the views of prison staff. London: Prison Reform Trust.

Quarmby, K. (2008) Getting Away with Murder: disabled people's experiences of hate crime in the UK, London: Scope, Disability Now and the United Kingdom's Disabled Peoples' Council.